MW01445584

The **Giant Book** of **TINY HOMES**

LIVING LARGE IN SMALL SPACES

JOHN RIHA

CENTENNIAL BOOKS

The Giant Book of TINY HOMES

LIVING LARGE IN SMALL SPACES

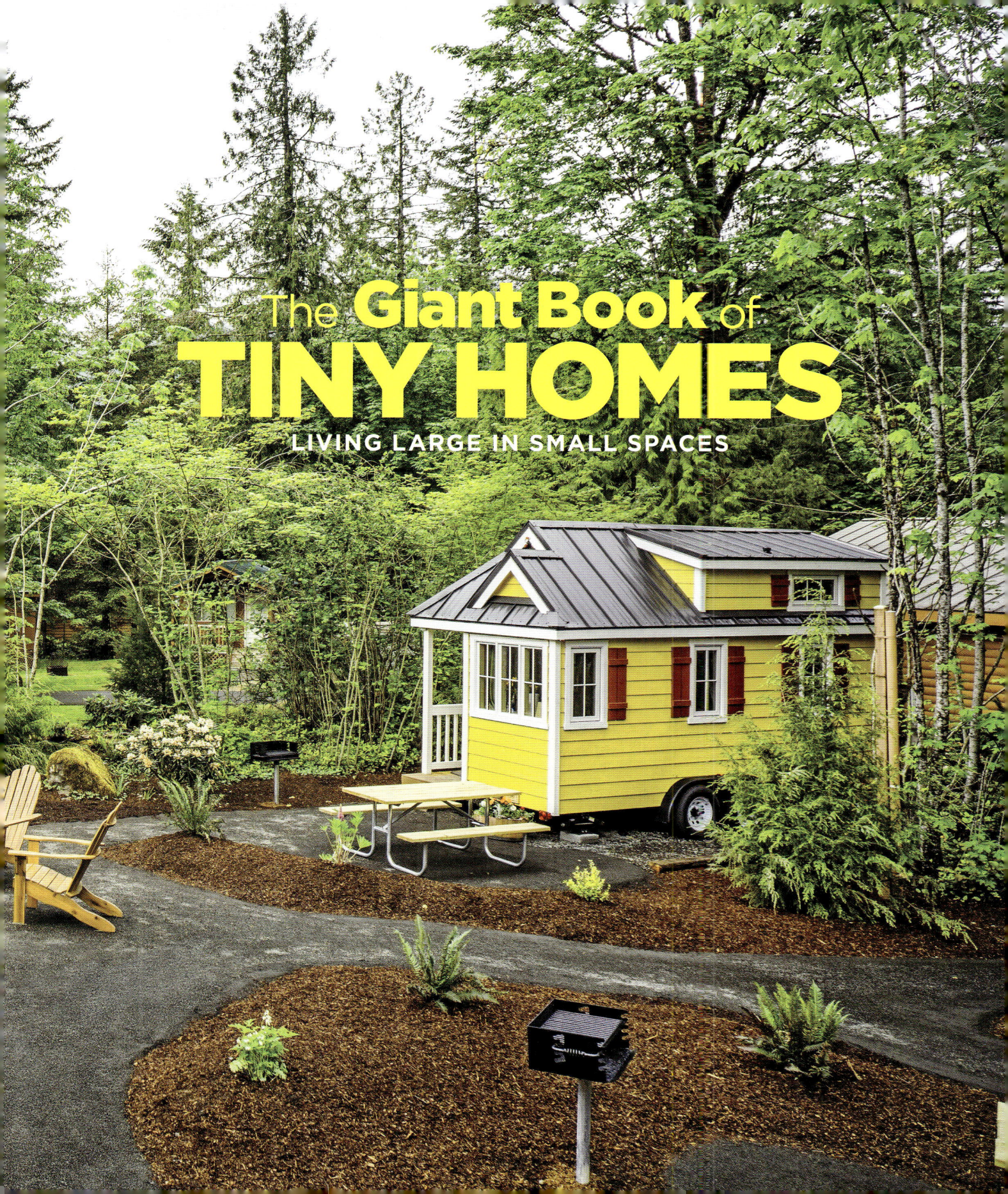

contents

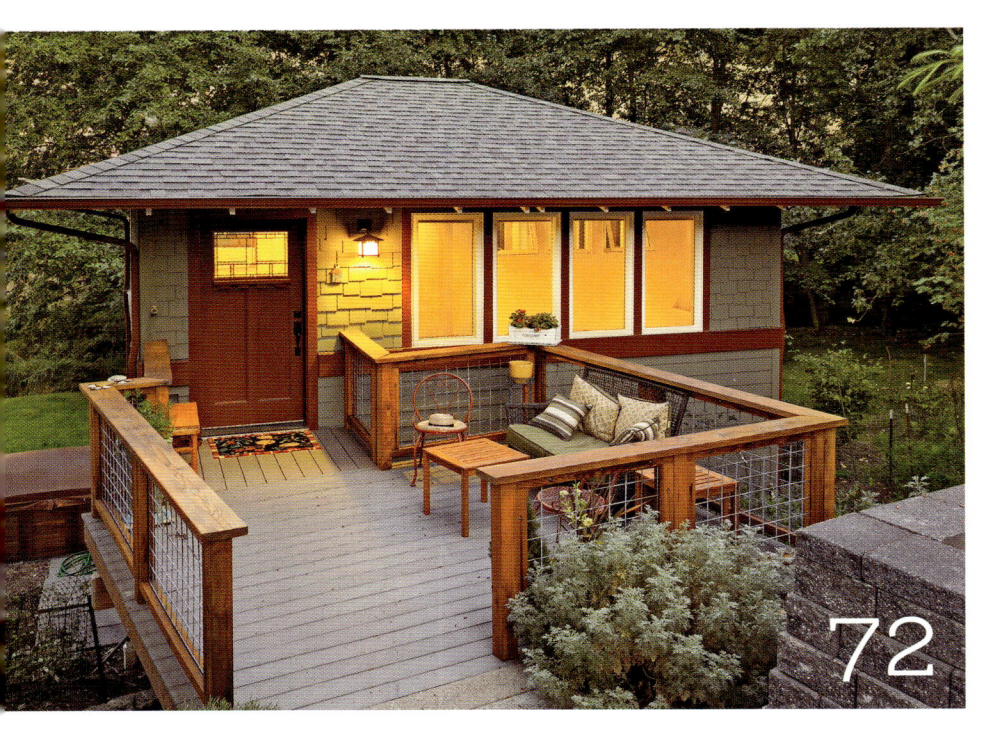

72

6 **INTRODUCTION**
Why you may want to live large in a tiny house.

CHAPTER 1
GOING TINY

10 **ENCYCLOPEDIA OF SMALL HOMES**
A rundown of common terms used in the world of small houses.

16 **5 QUESTIONS TO ASK BEFORE GOING SMALL**
Do you have the right mindset for tiny living?

20 **CODES & ZONING**
What you need to know before building or buying.

24 **LIVING TINY AS A FAMILY**
How one mom stays sane with two kids, a partner and a Great Dane in a 232-square-foot house.

30 **PLANNING A SMALL-SPACE KITCHEN**
There's no need to sacrifice convenience in this all-important room.

36 **BUILDING CODES MAKE BETTER BATHROOMS**
Tips for adding both function and beauty to your toilet and bath.

40 **STORAGE HACKS**
Squeeze in more stuff without having to sacrifice your space.

CHAPTER 2
SMALL HOMES ON FOUNDATIONS

46 **SMALLER THAN SMALL**
These homeowners went from 672 square feet to 330—and love it.

52 **GREENER LIVING IN A SMALL SPACE**
Occupying a scaled-down footprint can have an outsize influence on the environment.

60 **COTTAGE CLASSIC**
A New England getaway is defined by its focus on details.

66 **FARMHOUSE REDUX**
Texas style is at the heart of the design of a modular-built country house.

72 **SWEET DREAMING**
For an Oregon homeowner, it all began with a vision.

134

4 THE GIANT BOOK OF TINY HOMES

94

78 **WAY OUTSIDE THE BOX**
A prefab house fits in perfectly amid the New Hampshire landscape.

86 **SAVING FACE**
Restoring a charming 1940s California cottage in Laguna Beach.

CHAPTER 3
GOING MOBILE

94 **SUPER-SMALL ME**
At less than 150 square feet, this über-cute home is big on style and ready to roll.

100 **GIANT JOURNEY**
A woman, a dog and a tiny house on wheels make a heartfelt 25,000-mile trek.

108 **DIY TINY**
A Portland, Oregon, couple learns to build a downsize home for themselves on a budget.

114 **CHARLESTONIAN DREAMING**
A South Carolina home draws on a historic look.

CHAPTER 4
BACKWOODS BEAUTIES

122 **BRANCHING OUT**
One enterprising builder turns boyhood dreams of treehouses into grown-up realities.

128 **SWEET SALVAGE**
A Texas builder uses recycled and reclaimed materials to build his rustic cabins.

134 **ROCK STAR**
A secluded home with a limited footprint offers its own unique set of challenges.

140 **SERENITY AT EAGLE POINT**
A simple design amid panoramic views provides a haven of peace and quiet in Washington state.

144 **THE BOOTSTRAPPERS**
Beauty meets practicality in a scenic, eastern Washington abode.

152 **REMOTE POSSIBILITY**
A Canadian retreat offers uninterrupted vistas.

CHAPTER 5
THE TINY HOME LIFE

160 **BEST PLANTS FOR SMALL SPACES**
How to bring the outdoors inside with greenery.

162 **MAKING THE MOST OF A TINY GARDEN**
You can still get big yields from a small, backyard-garden plot.

164 **THROWING A (TINY) DINNER PARTY**
Savvy ways to entertain big, even when living in a small-scale home.

168 **OFF THE GRID**
Get the essentials of heat, water and power before you unplug.

176 **STAYING TOASTY IN EXTREME COLD**
Innovative ways to help keep warm when the outdoor temps dip.

178 **WHERE TO GO TINY**
Whether it's for a few nights or a long-term commitment, here's where you can live small.

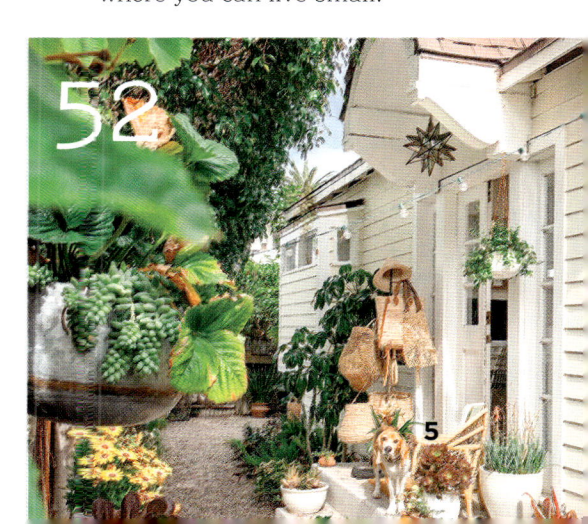

52

INTRODUCTION

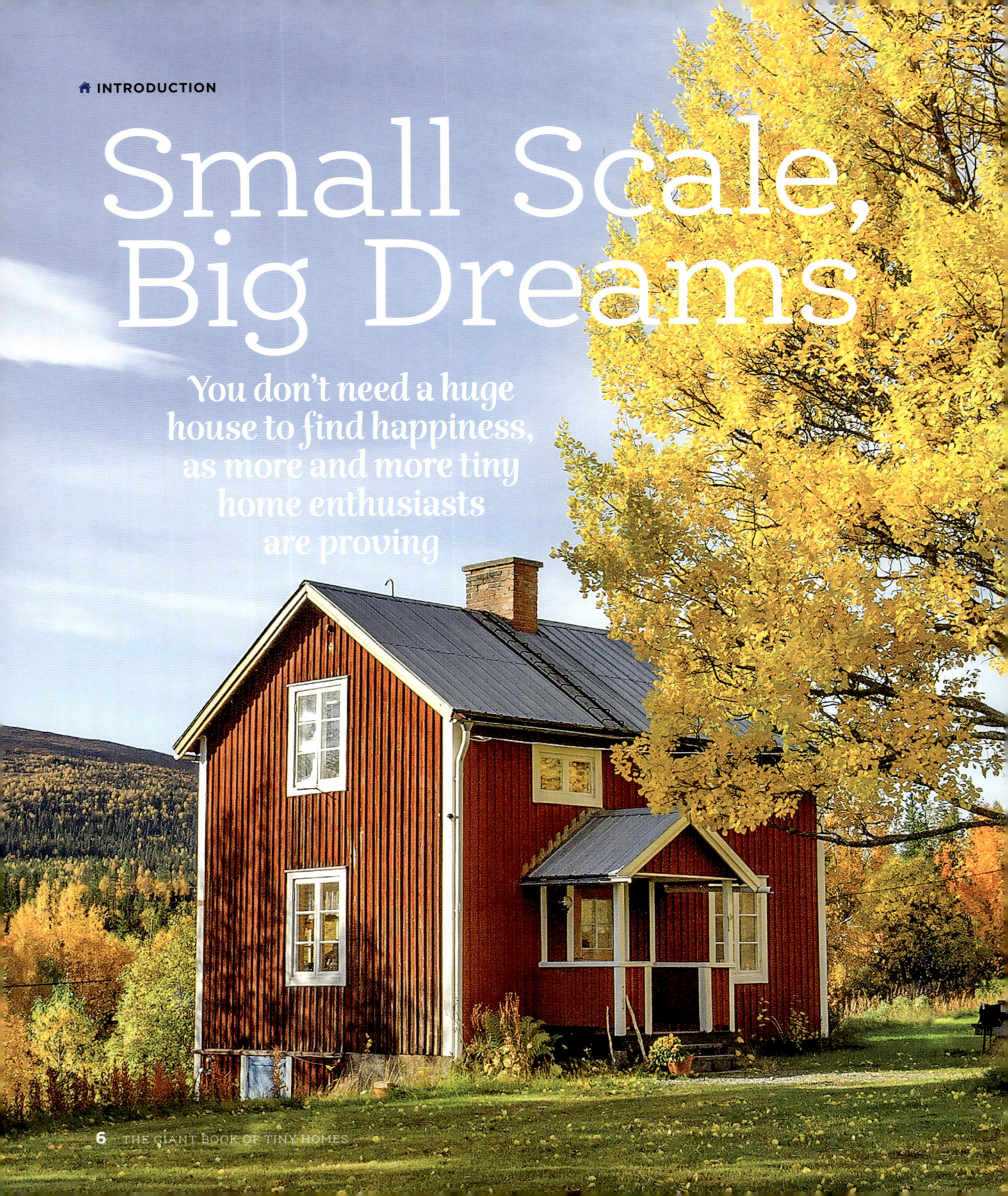

Small Scale, Big Dreams

You don't need a huge house to find happiness, as more and more tiny home enthusiasts are proving

Our home environments are constantly changing. Innovations, new products and smart design ideas are helping our houses become more comfortable, safe, stylish and personable.

But one of the biggest changes in recent years is actually the smallest. Many of today's homeowners are intrigued by the idea of downsizing—living in smaller, more affordable homes that are less expensive to buy and easier to maintain than larger houses; along with the extra work they often bring.

Although there's no magic formula for what qualifies a house as "tiny," there's no doubt that downsizing embraces values that many people find attractive and meaningful. For example, overall consumption is reduced—fewer building materials are needed for construction, less furniture is required to fill smaller spaces and limited storage space dictates that items like artwork, kitchen utensils and even clothing must be pared to essentials. Although daunting at first, the act of reducing possessions can be liberating, both financially and spiritually.

Upfront, buying a small house usually means a lower capital investment, so financing is easier to obtain, property taxes are minimalized, and monthly mortgage payments are less of a burden. Well-insulated smaller homes use less power to heat and cool, lowering utility costs. There's less time spent on upkeep, such as painting siding and cleaning floors and windows.

Reducing costs translates to less stress—and who doesn't want that? In addition, saving time on everyday chores means more time for you: more time to devote to your family, an entrepreneurial business, or simply relaxing. In our modern, hectic world, a lifestyle with less stress and more discretionary time can be liberating.

Best of all, architects, designers and builders are paying close attention to the tiny house movement and responding with small houses that maximize efficiency while sacrificing nothing in the way of style and convenience. Whether your taste runs to traditional houses or leans toward something more exotic, such as a house on wheels or even a fully functioning house built in the trees, *The Giant Book of Tiny Homes* is full of beautiful examples and savvy ideas that will inspire your creativity and put a smile on your face. Welcome to the big world of living tiny!

—John Riha

COME ON IN! Tiny home communities are growing across the U.S., offering shared common spaces and a welcoming vibe.

CHAPTER 1

Going Tiny

Scaled-down spaces don't mean compromising your desire to think big

GOING TINY

Encyclopedia of Small Homes

Terms for types of houses abound—here's what you need to know

STAY SAVVY: KNOWING THE CURRENT TERMS IS ESPECIALLY HELPFUL IF YOU'RE DISCUSSING BUYING OR BUILDING BY PHONE OR EMAIL.

GIMME SHELTER
Tiny homes come in a variety of shapes, forms and sizes with an emphasis on getting more from less.

"Small home" is a subjective definition that's definitely in the eye of the beholder. Although the U.S. Census Bureau identifies the median size of the U.S. single-family residence at 2,422 square feet, most builders and architects will likely say a truly small house is defined as 1,000 square feet or less. That size puts the emphasis on clever design and construction.

Many zoning laws and building codes require a minimum square footage of 1,000 square feet for newly built homes set on permanent foundations. Although those restrictions are changing as municipalities become more small-house friendly, you should definitely check with your local planning department about minimum sizes before buying or building. In rural areas, such regulations are less likely, and getaway cabins are often smaller than the 1,000-square-foot minimum.

Small home construction methods can be confusing, and there are terms that are often used interchangeably, even if they have different meanings. Here's a rundown of a few key terms that may be helpful to know:

Accessory Dwelling Unit (ADU)

ADU or accessory dwelling unit is a legal term for a separate second apartment or house that includes its own entrance, kitchen, bathroom and sleeping area. An ADU shares the building lot of a larger main house. An ADU may be a separate building or attached to an existing house or garage. It usually shares the utility connections of the larger house, and it often serves as a rental unit or as housing for a family member.

During the housing boom that followed World War II, many residential areas were zoned to limit density and ensure space between houses, especially in the fast-growing suburbs. However, in recent years those regulations have been relaxed as cities and surrounding communities attempt to limit urban sprawl. Many municipalities have relaxed regulations regarding the minimum size of building lots, and zoning laws have changed to permit more ADUs. These new laws generally have restrictions on the style and size of ADUs, and most require that the property owner also reside on the property.

GOING TINY

Granny Pod
Granny pod is a generic term for an accessory dwelling unit that's intended for an aging parent to live in close proximity to a relative or caregiving friend. Although not a legal description, many ADUs can be designed specifically as "granny pods," with ergonomically friendly design, barrier-free bathrooms and generous lighting.

Manufactured
Manufactured housing is completely created in a factory, with no on-site construction. These homes are built on wheels, transported to the property site, then fitted onto a foundation. The trailer parks that date back to the 1960s and '70s largely feature manufactured housing. Today, new designs and construction methods are helping remove some of the stigma that comes with manufactured housing, since it's one of the cheapest forms of residential living.

Mobile
Mobile home is another term for a manufactured house that's built on a permanent chassis so it can be transported. However, it typically isn't moved once it's placed on a lot. Mobile homes must be built to certain federal construction standards determined by the U.S. Department of Housing and Urban Development, known as HUD Title VI standards. A compliant mobile home must display documentation known as a "data plate" inside and a "certification label" on the back end of the house. Removal of these documents is illegal, and they can't be replaced.

Modular
Modular houses are factory-built in whole, boxlike sections. At the job site, the boxes are lifted into place with a crane and then fastened together to form the complete house. They can be stacked on top of each other to form multistory houses or they may be fitted side-by-side. Because the modules must be transported by flatbed truck to the job site, they are limited to being no more than 16 feet wide—the legal "oversize load" width limit for highways. However, a good modular design model ensures that these types of houses can be customized to suit the buyer's individualized requirements.

> THE WORLD OF SMALL HOMES IS EVER-CHANGING, AND REGULATIONS ARE UNDER CONSTANT REVISION.

MAINTAIN INDEPENDENCE
Granny pods are increasingly popular for families who want to have aging relatives stay in close proximity.

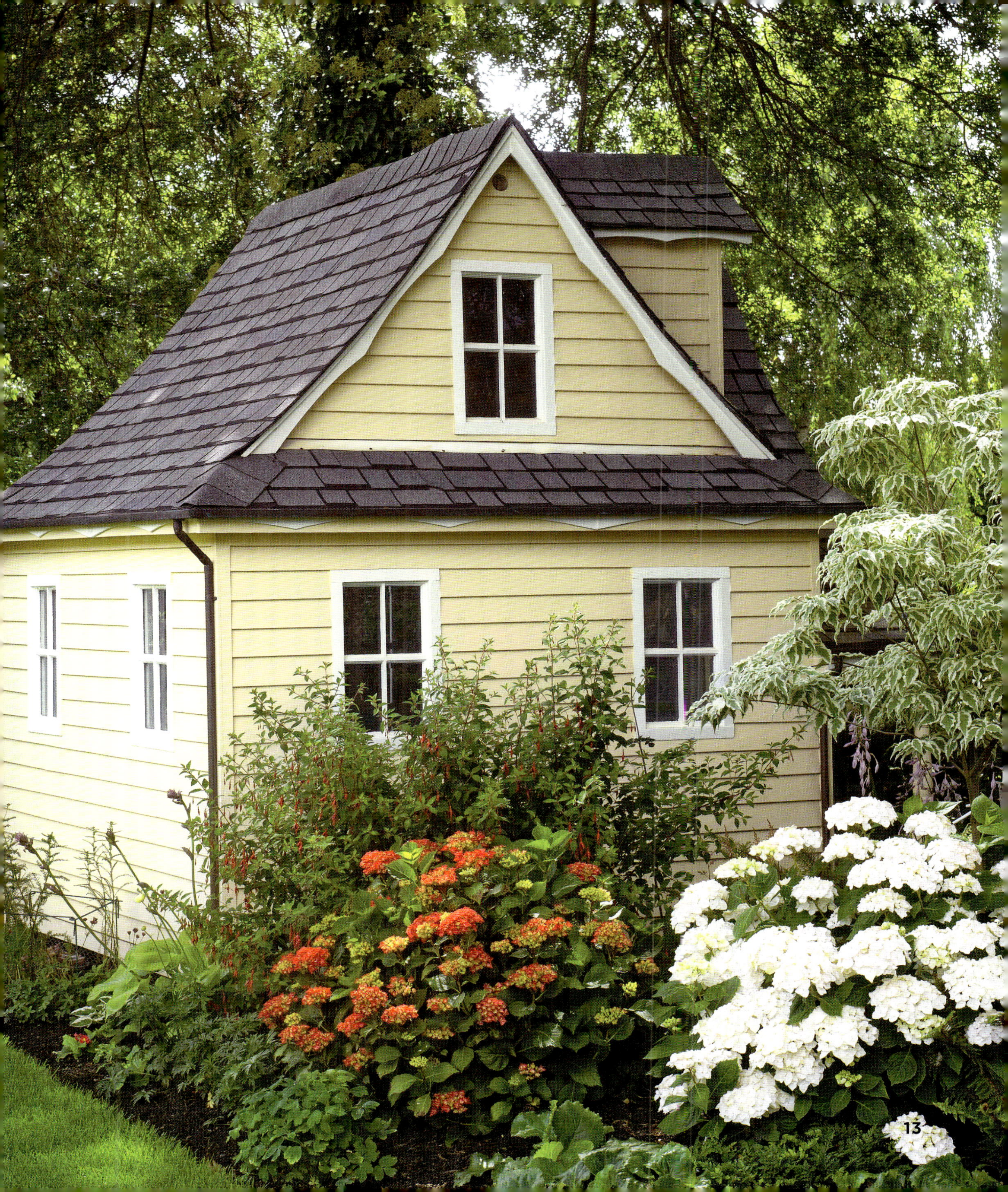

GOING TINY

Panel-Built
Panel-built houses are constructed as separate pieces—walls, floors and roofs are factory-built then shipped to the job site to be assembled. Another term for panel-built housing is "flat-pack," because the finished walls and floors are stacked on top of each other for easy transport. The degree of finish of each piece varies with the manufacturer. Some have cabinets, fixtures and other components already installed; others ship them separately and have them installed on-site.

Prefab
Prefab is a generic term for any house or structure that's built in a factory and then assembled at the job site. Both "modular" and "panel-built" houses are prefab types of homes. All prefabricated houses must meet local and federal building codes and pass regular inspections, just like any conventionally built house.

RV
Recreational vehicle or RV is a broad term that covers many types of vehicles used for traveling and exploration by road. RV is often used interchangeably with the word "motor home," but motor home is an informal name, while "recreational vehicle" is a technical term with legal regulations and restrictions. There are several classifications of RVs:

THE GIANT BOOK OF TINY HOMES

PARK IT
Though they make great getaway cabins, state and local regulations may limit how long you can keep THOWs in one location.

CLASS A recreational vehicles generally are large, well-appointed mobile homes with generous living and bedrooms and full bathrooms. Class A includes buses that have been converted into RVs.

CLASS B recreational vehicles are single-chassis vehicles and include vans modified with raised roofs, small kitchens and sleeping accommodations. Larger models may have a water heater, heat and air-conditioning and a toilet.

CLASS C recreational vehicles are distinguished by their distinct cab-over design. That design usually is for a sleeping berth that clears the way for more interior living space.

Tiny Houses on Wheels (THOWs)

Tiny houses on wheels, also called THOWs, are legally considered recreational vehicles or RVs. A tiny house on wheels should be registered with your state as an RV and can't have more than 400 square feet of living space. If you're traveling with your THOW, you don't have to worry about residential zoning laws, but you'll need to find a place to park it. You can put it on the property of a friend or family member—or property you own outright—but most states prohibit you from establishing a permanent residence.

You can put it in an RV park or a campground, but there are restrictions on how long you can stay. Keep checking, though: State and local regulations are slowly changing to allow variations in size limitations and permanent locations. ■

CLASS B VANS
Hit the open road and feed your wanderlust. Some vans have beds, kitchens and even (very small) bathrooms.

GOING TINY

Five Questions to Ask...

Before Going Small

If you're thinking of downsizing and living tiny, first have a heart-to-heart with yourself

If you like cozy spaces and the idea of living without lots of stuff, then a small home might be the perfect fit.

> SPEND SOME
> TIME CAREFULLY
> CONSIDERING WHAT
> IT WILL BE LIKE
> TO LIVE ON A
> SMALLER SCALE.

1

Is Downsizing Really Right for You?

The tiny house movement is big these days and getting a lot of attention. Many small houses are cuter than cute and understandably less expensive than larger houses with similar materials and finishes, and they can reduce a carbon footprint while lowering maintenance and utility costs.

Bob Knight, a Brooksville, Maine, architect who's designed small homes for 40 years, says many clients start off thinking they want an itsy-bitsy house and eventually expand their vision.

"They forget they all have this stuff," Knight says. "That's usually the thing that pushes small house design into bigger spaces." To avoid downsizing shock, try living in a small house for a week or more. If possible, shoot for a rainy week, when going outside isn't practical—that should give you a good idea of whether small confines agree with your nature. Some tiny home communities and manufacturers also make rentals available for vacationers and prospective homeowners. Or try searching vacation rental sites, like Vrbo or Airbnb, for small houses that will give you a taste of living tiny (for ideas, see page 178).

2

What's Your Budget?

Small doesn't necessarily come cheap. Building a custom house with first-class materials, finishes and appliances may cost $300 per square foot or more. Sure, frugal strategizing can lower some of your overall costs, and obviously a smaller footprint can mean fewer building materials and ultimately a less-expensive place to build or buy. Many small home owners proudly declare that they've paid off a mortgage in short order. But the cautionary tale here is that, as with any major project or purchase, careful budgeting and cost estimating is paramount, no matter what size your dream home may be.

GOING TINY

3

How Tiny Can You Go?

NASA, which has been pondering colonizing Mars, investigated how much habitable space a human needs during a space mission and came up with 883 cubic feet per person. For perspective: A typical tiny house on wheels that meets road limit requirements—12 feet tall, 8.5 feet wide and 26 feet long—contains about 2,650 cubic feet of space. Take away cabinets, furnishings, appliances and unused overhead space, and you easily cut that volume in half.

If you're flying your tiny house solo to Mars, that space might feel luxurious. But an Earthbound couple may find that amount of space less than ideal. Good house design, however, can help make small spaces feel larger:

- **High ceilings** add volume.
- **Generous windows** and skylights open up interiors and help flood smaller rooms with light.
- **Convertible, multifunctional furnishings** help you get maximum use out of small areas.
- **Well-insulated homes** can be heated with a single gas fireplace or baseboard heaters and cooled with a mini-split air conditioner. That can eliminate bulky ductwork and a mechanical room with a furnace or forced-air conditioner.

4

What Are Local Regulations?

When it comes to building and zoning codes, tiny homes "often fall through the cracks," says Kim Bucciero, CFO of the MicroLife Institute in Atlanta.

The International Residential Code (IRC), which most municipalities adopt as their local building code, states that rooms in one- and two-family houses (except bathrooms and kitchens) must be at least 70 square feet with ceiling heights of 7 feet. In 2015, a tiny home appendix was added to the IRC that relaxes these restrictions, although not a lot of municipalities use it yet.

Zoning laws are trickier. Most places in the country don't allow you to build and live in a "tiny house" as the principal dwelling on a piece of land—although that is slowly changing as the tiny home grassroots movement pressures zoning boards to start thinking about accommodating smaller residences that help make housing more affordable.

5

Can You Take Advantage of Outdoor Space?

Outside takes on an oversize importance when you live in a small home. Many small-space dwellers add porches and decks that add low-cost livability; others join communities of tiny homes grouped together to enjoy outdoor communal activities.

Think about your year-round climate and temperature before you go small. An agreeably mild climate can increase opportunities for outdoor living, helping to expand your living area. ■

THINK BIG
For a more expansive feel, consider employing skylights and large windows.

18 THE GIANT BOOK OF TINY HOMES

WHEN THE WEATHER COOPERATES, THERE'S A LOT YOU CAN DO IN AN OUTDOOR SPACE.

BE CREATIVE
From rooftop patios to front stoop decor, access to the outdoors makes any dwelling feel bigger.

GOING TINY

Codes & Zoning

There are different regulations depending on what type of tiny home you want to live in

🏠 GOING TINY

Building codes and zoning ordinances have major impacts on how houses are built and occupied in this country. If you don't understand the laws, it's easy to end up with an illegal structure. Codes dictate how a structure is built, while zoning outlines where a house may be placed.

When it comes to tiny houses, most people focus on whether a house is movable or not. The more important question is whether you're planning a recreational vehicle (RV) that you'll take on the road frequently or a house.

If the plan is to build a tiny house RV, then the codes to consider are American National Standards Institute (ANSI) 119.5 and National Fire Protection Association (NFPA) 1192. These standards are more lenient than residential

• • •

KNOWING WHAT TYPE OF STRUCTURE IS DESIRED BECOMES ESSENTIAL WHEN CONSIDERING ZONING ORDINANCES.

• • •

construction codes; however, the typical end result is not a primary residence. Furthermore, the overseeing body—the Recreational Vehicle Industry Association (RVIA)—does not allow owner-builds.

If your plan is to build a tiny house, then the International Residential Code (IRC) should be used. The "*2018 IRC Appendix Q: Tiny Houses*," which I co-authored with Martin Hammer, was adopted into the 2018 IRC building code and provides essential information for anyone interested in building a tiny house. It affords special provisions for common challenges found in tiny houses such as ceiling heights, loft usage and access, room size and emergency egress.

Knowing what type of structure you want (tiny house or tiny house RV) is essential when you're considering zoning ordinances. Tiny house RVs aren't legal for permanent occupancy in most residential zones because they're considered recreational housing. On the other hand, a tiny

STAYING PUT
A tiny house that will be your primary residence must follow a stricter building code.

ROLL OUT
Tiny house RVs offer the freedom of easy movement.

house can be built in residential zoning as long as it: 1) is a dwelling built to IRC standards and 2) the zoning allows for small structures. Because zoning requirements can limit design options, it's important to understand your local zoning laws before buying land and building.

This topic is often considered confusing; however, if you do a little research, you'll understand the distinction between a tiny house and a tiny house RV. It's important that you know whether you want a house or RV before the structure is designed. Talk to your planning department about zoning and code requirements. If your goal is to be mobile, then build a tiny house RV using ANSI or NFPA standards. If you want to construct a primary residence, then build under the guidance of the IRC. —Andrew Morrison

Andrew Morrison is a 20-year veteran in the building industry and an expert in the field of tiny house construction. Find plans and videos at TinyHouseBuild.com.

What a Tiny House Is Legally NOT:

- **Manufactured Housing** Manufactured houses are overseen by HUD (U.S. Department of Housing and Urban Development), which doesn't govern tiny houses.

- **Recreational Vehicle (RV)** Tiny houses used for frequent travel fall into this category; however, if the end product is a house (primary residence), then it cannot be an RV in most jurisdictions.

- **Park Model** These are legally considered to be recreational housing and cannot be used as primary residences in most jurisdictions.

GOING TINY

Living Tiny as a Family

With a partner, two kids and a dog, this mom knows how to make contentedness the biggest part of a small space

THE GOOD LIFE
Macy Miller, seven months pregnant, enjoys the outdoor patio with her partner, James Herndon, and daughter, Hazel.

Let's get one thing straight: "Going tiny" is not about the house. Tiny homes can be cute, but that isn't enough. It's about adapting to a different lifestyle. It's definitely not easy. In fact, it takes effort and persistence to make it work. But that juice is well worth the squeeze!

I've "lived tiny" for more than six years. I started off as just a girl and her dog. Eventually my partner, James, moved in, and we had a daughter, Hazel. Our second child, Miles, was born after these photos were taken. Together, the five of us live in our 232-square-foot tiny house—at one point we even downsized to a more mobile 84-square-foot, custom-designed and self-built micro house. In those tight quarters, you can bet I've learned a fair bit about how to successfully navigate small spaces, particularly with other people.

Like most parents, our young kids are our priority. That puts me mostly at home, with multiple people, in tight quarters. Also, we live where winter means snow, so we're inside a lot. There's a phrase that gets thrown around regarding people who live in tiny homes—"they spend most of their time outside." It's just not true for us, yet we're still alive to talk about it! Sure, living tiny isn't all rainbows and unicorns—although we do have a toilet made of glitter!

ROOM TO SPARE
Pullout toy drawers beneath a pair of built-in bunk beds make an efficient storage space for all the kids' toys.

25

🏠 GOING TINY

> CONNECT WITH OTHER TINY HOUSE PARENTS VIA BLOGS AND SOCIAL MEDIA TO SHARE SUPPORT, TIPS AND LAUGHS.

ALL IN ONE
The compact galley kitchen includes a space-saving dual clothes washer/dryer. The sleeping loft is tucked neatly behind the media wall of the living room.

26 THE GIANT BOOK OF TINY HOMES

COME ON IN!
The main door accesses the nearby street. Beneath the towing arm, a hidden storage closet stashes outdoor tools.

Here are some truths I've learned living tiny as a family:

It's Going to Make or Break Relationships

The actual day-to-day living in a tiny house is not hard as a single person, a couple or a family. What is hard is meaningful relationships. That small space doesn't give you a lot of room to ignore any work that needs to be done on your relationships. There's no space to storm off and develop a grudge. You can try, but eventually you'll have to get rid of the elephants in the room and learn to work through your trouble spots, together. I've found this happens much faster in a small space where you can't hide very long. For a lot of people, that may feel like a deal-breaker. If you're up for it, though, I believe it leads to more meaningful and impactful relationships.

You'll Have More Spare Time, Even With Kids!

You will save so much time cleaning and maintaining fewer rooms and less stuff that one day it may hit you that you're sitting still and actually enjoying a hot cup of coffee. The idea of hot coffee is more than enough payback for me at this toddler stage, but that precious extra time might also give you more opportunity to enjoy family hobbies together, reading good books, camping, hiking and exploring, or maybe even playing sports. Our family spends a lot of time painting and learning music together because we can all have fun at our different levels, and I want creativity to be at the foundation of what we do.

Quality time is invaluable for creating strong family bonds. Having more free time also makes those moments less stressful and more impactful.

🏠 GOING TINY

A DOG'S LIFE
The perfect pooch for a small space? It's Denver the Great Dane, of course!

You Might Have More Money— or You Might Not

When you cut your square footage, you can also cut your mortgage—maybe completely—and you'll drastically cut your utilities. Our cooling bill went from several hundred dollars every summer to about a hundred bucks, and savings on heating is even more dramatic. That means the majority of your paycheck isn't already allocated somewhere by the time it's in your hands. Instead, you get to choose to save or to spend on things like family vacations, events, concerts and classes. Or, like me, you may opt to quit your day job to spend that time with your family instead.

Your Kids Don't Need That Much Stuff!

We never had a baby registry. My kids didn't use bumpers, bouncers or any blinky things at home. Instead, we aimed to unbusy our life enough to be the rocker, the bouncer and the seat as needed. We both wanted to be very hands-on, which required us to get hands-off about other things.

OPEN UP
A sliding "barn-style" door to the bathroom saves space. The hallway leads to the children's bedroom.

It wasn't easy, but we made it through babyhood with only a car seat, some blankets and clothes to keep warm, and some milk for their bellies.

As my kids grow, I'm constantly worried if I'm providing enough. Then we visit other parents. Again and again we hear how toys never get played with until another kid is there to play, too. It seems to me that interaction is where the fun is for kids, and maybe even the education. So we continue to primarily cut out the "middleman" and make time to frequent public play spaces for peer interaction.

We do have a select few toys at home, which we reassess often to see whether they are adding to or distracting from life. Sometimes we see a child playing with a fun toy and it's definitely adorable. But it's times like those when we're grateful we don't have the space at home to justify pulling out our wallet for a splurge. In a way, our tiny house supports our goals even when we feel like diverting momentarily.

Parenting Is Still a Challenge
Parenting is hard. But that has nothing to do with the size of your house. We've found the smaller space has really helped us become better communicators by allowing us to slow down as needed and encouraging interaction. I think this relationship dance is very important for sustaining family bonds and for teaching children how to handle emotions. To be frank, handling emotions was something I never had to be very good at until our tiny house forced me to acknowledge them.

I'm Probably Going to Mess My Kids Up Anyway
Tiny houses aren't a golden ticket through parenthood, but I feel they've added immensely to our family's quality of life. We own our life choices and make decisions based on our values. Living tiny has not always been an easy choice, but it's one we continue to make every day because it helps us lead an extraordinary lifestyle that is intentional and that I hope continues to be impactful to us and our kids.

Living tiny has provided us freedom from debt, meaningful relationships with time to enjoy them and the ability to pursue our own passions. We see amazing places together and experience our days thoroughly. We've learned when and how to take our own space on those other days. I joke that my kids will probably rebel and find themselves eventually living in huge homes. As long as they are happy, so am I, because life is about so much more than a house. But a house can definitely support your family values and help enable a better life! —Macy Miller

🏠 GOING TINY

YOU WON'T REGRET HAVING A BIG WINDOW IN YOUR KITCHEN THAT LETS IN LOTS OF DAYLIGHT AND MAKES FOOD PREP EASY.

Planning a Small-Space Kitchen

Focus on priorities, and you'll still have the culinary castle of your dreams

In a compact area, you can probably afford to splurge on nice surfaces, like subway tile.

GOING TINY

Combo washer/dryer appliances save plenty of space.

CLIMB ON BOARD
Loft stairways offer lots of room underneath for appliances, storage cubbies and hanging message boards.

Some walk-in closets may be bigger than your kitchen. But the thing is, no matter your layout—horseshoe, L-shape, galley or single wall—you can work with limited square footage to create a beautiful, small cooking space that's highly functional and enjoyable to use.

What is the trick to getting it right? "Being honest about what you need so you can plan accordingly," says tiny home builder Hannah Rose Crabtree of Pocket Mansions in west Seattle. While larger kitchens have the room to be multifunctional hubs for everything from cooking to entertaining and binge-watching, you have to prioritize function in a small cooking space. "And to do that, you've got to nail down your kitchen essentials," Crabtree says.

For instance, if you're a dedicated home chef, a high-end range might be a must. Don't cook much but need a place for the kids to do homework? Squeezing in a kitchen island or peninsula with tuck-away stools may top your list.

Make Room for the Right Equipment

Many manufacturers offer slimmer alternatives to standard-size kitchen appliances, typically knocking off about six inches (and sometimes more) from the width. For example: Don't have room for a standard 24-inch-wide dishwasher? Consider an 18-inch model. Can't fit a 36-inch refrigerator? A 24-incher to the rescue! Even fixtures such as sinks are available in smaller-than-usual sizes. Depending on your needs, blending smaller appliances and fixtures into your kitchen design mix may give you the room for the full-size features you just have to have.

When Devon Loftus, the founder of Moon Cycle Bakery in Olympia, Washington, was designing her 18-square-foot galley kitchen from scratch, she made a few compromises to squeeze in a full-size oven. "I gave up some countertop space and installed an apartment-size refrigerator that is smaller than a standard 36-inch model," she says.

How did Loftus make up for the lost prep space? "My husband and I created designated zones in the kitchen for specific tasks, so someone had a place to chop while the other was working the stove." Keeping the classic kitchen triangle in mind helped. Loftus placed the stove, refrigerator and sink at opposite points but still within easy reach

⌂ GOING TINY

PLAN AHEAD
Design counters and storage cubbies so you can tuck stools underneath when not in use. Add shelves to high walls for extra storage.

of the food prep area to help maximize efficiency while they were working.

Maximize Space With Custom Cabinetry

"Small spaces require extra attention to detail," says interior designer Dawn D Totty of Nashville, Tennessee. "Embracing the concept of 'every square inch counts' at the forefront of your design choices will ensure the best and most functional result."

A movable kitchen island is one of her favorite space-saving tricks. "Even in large cooking spaces, homeowners are opting for smaller custom islands with casters that can be moved or relocated as a serving station in other spots of the home," Totty says.

She also suggests splurging on custom cabinets—storage tailored to your needs and space will improve flow in your kitchen. To avoid visual clutter, keep the look minimal with plain, flat-front cabinetry and little detailing.

Maximizing vertical space also helps, Totty adds. If you install upper cabinets that reach to the ceiling, they will draw your eye upward while adding much-needed storage space.

Open concept shelving is not just one of the top trends, it's also a great way to dress up a kitchen by showcasing your best dishes, Totty says. Even better, the shelving is cheaper than installing upper cabinets.

Personalize Your Kitchen

Flooring and backsplashes can be beautiful focal points that add pattern, texture and color to small cooking spaces. "My favorite ways for personalizing a pint-size kitchen is by choosing beautiful tile and unique decorative lighting," says Paula Kinney, the lead designer at Love Your Nest Kitchen Design Studio in Euclid, Ohio. Sticking with large tiles or wide planks will make your small space appear larger.

A beautiful countertop is a great way to accessorize smartly, according to Teal Brown, owner of Wishbone Tiny Homes in Asheville, North Carolina. A durable stone countertop will bring a splash of luxury to the space, but if it's out of your budget, a butcher-block counter is a practical alternative that looks great and is affordable, to boot. ■

HANG-UPS
Open wall space with rods and hooks let you hang kitchen utensils and cutting boards right where you need them.

GOING TINY

Building Codes
Make Better Bathrooms

Knowing the rules gives your compact lavatory functionality and safety without compromising style

SHOP SMALL
Mini-size fixtures made for half baths give you all the functionality of full-size fixtures.

NEED ADVICE? CHECK ONLINE BOOKSELLERS FOR PLANNING GUIDELINES FROM THE NATIONAL KITCHEN & BATH ASSOCIATION (NKBA).

Trying to fit all the essential features into a super-small bathroom can feel like a clown-car gag minus the laughter. What's the biggest head-scratcher? Understanding how building codes can impact your design decisions.

Regulations are put in place by local and state governments, and you shouldn't ignore them, says Dawn D Totty, a Nashville, Tennessee, interior designer. She adds, "While they may seem like a nuisance, they exist to protect people from injury and homes from damage." For example, electrical codes for shower lighting prevent electrocution and fire.

It's also critical to know that residential codes can vary from county to county within a state. "But there are rules of thumb that dictate form and function that are pretty universal," says New York City architect John Mochelle. "These are typically measurements established to boost

● ● ●

BUILDING CODES AREN'T THERE TO GET IN YOUR WAY—THEY'RE FOR SAFETY, AND THEY CAN BE VALUABLE RESOURCES FOR CREATING COMFORTABLE, LIVABLE SPACES.

● ● ●

usability, so you do not wind up with a bathroom that is awkward to use. For instance, clearance requirements for toilets typically include a minimum of 21 inches in front for doing your business comfortably."

What kind of homes should adhere to building codes? "Think permanent, immobile buildings like houses and apartments. Towable dwellings like

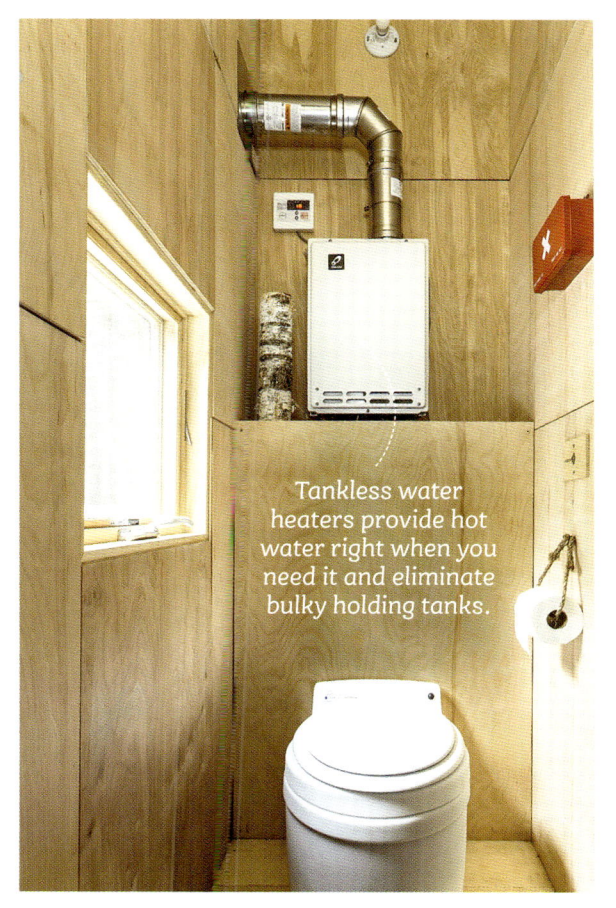

Low-cost galvanized steel panels shed water and won't rust.

Tankless water heaters provide hot water right when you need it and eliminate bulky holding tanks.

37

GOING TINY

recreational vehicles have their own unique set of standards for road insurance," says Mochelle.

Fixes for Common Small-Space Problems

After designing dozens of small bathrooms, Sherry Gosset, the lead designer at Showcase Kitchens based in Manhasset, New York, has picked up many tricks for making the most of itty-bitty spaces.

Don't have enough clearance inside your bathroom for a traditional door? "Install a pocket door or sliding barn door," says Gosset. "If neither option works for your budget, consider reversing the door swing." Another idea worth borrowing is ditching a wall radiator for radiant heating installed under the floor. She loves this idea because it can free up precious inches for a different bathroom feature.

Just like toilets, bathroom vanities require 21 inches of clearance in front. For those times when a standard model is just too big to squeeze in, Newell Slade, contractor and owner of Newell Building in Casa Grande, Arizona, will turn to a specialty store such as IKEA for a shallow solution. "You can also opt for a slim pedestal sink and then go vertical with wall-mounted storage," he says.

"The minimum measurement for a shower floor is 30 inches by 30 inches," says Mochelle. While you could install a builder-grade shower box that uses a curtain, he suggests splurging on a frameless glass stall. "It is my favorite trick for creating visual space because the borderless glass walls do not obstruct views or light—two things needed to make a minuscule bathroom feel open and airy instead of cramped and dark." ∎

CLEAN-UP
Compact vanities include a sink, single-lever faucet, countertop and storage space.

ALL TOGETHER
An all-in-one bath has a sink faucet attached to a flexible pullout supply tube that doubles as a showerhead.

THE GIANT BOOK OF TINY HOMES

PREFER A TUB OVER A SHOWER? STANDARD TUBS ARE 60 INCHES IN LENGTH, BUT YOU CAN FIND SOAKING TUBS THAT ARE 48 INCHES AND LESS.

MIXED UP
Different finishes, such as this tile and wood-panel bath, helps a small space look and feel larger. Big mirrors help reflect light.

GOING TINY

Storage Hacks

Looking to squeeze in just a bit more space for some gotta-haves? Here are ideas to help max out your mini crib

Simple DIY shelves come in all sizes to fit odd spaces.

WICKER BASKETS underneath a cozy daybed (left) add handy pullout storage, look great and are cheaper than slide-out drawers. You can find wicker baskets for $20 to $50.

SMALL NOOKS and wall indentations (above) are opportunities to add shelves for knickknacks, overflow books and quick-grab writing supplies.

DON'T FORGET DOORWAYS! There's often unused space right above the opening, especially in hallways. Add a shelf to hold decorative treasures, towels and household supplies.

WALL-RACK SYSTEMS make walls superfunctional. Store everything from kitchen utensils to herb plantings. An easy-care semigloss paint helps if a little wall cleanup is needed. You'll generally pay $20 to $150 for a rack and hooks.

GOING TINY

Pullout drawers under a stairwell keep everything at hand.

CHALK PAINT gives dual purpose to your wall storage. Write notes, reminders and sweet nothings. Find it for about $15 for 8 ounces at your local craft store or online.

PULLOUT DRAWERS are great for sneaking storage into smaller spaces. They put everything right where you can see it—no more reaching into a dark cubby to find the peppercorns. DIY drawer kits range from $15 to $100 per drawer.

UNDER-STAIRS STORAGE *(above)* is an organizational bonanza. That space can be fitted with drawers, shelves and cubbies. Some cabinet makers specialize in under-stairs solutions.

BARN-TYPE DOORS *(right)* slide out of the way and don't take up any floor space when they open and close. When they're open, they cover nearby walls, so choose a good-looking door. Glass doors help light reach inside small rooms. Barn door hardware ranges from $50 to several hundred dollars, so shop according to your budget.

A STEEL ROD over a sink, stove or countertop is a handy place to hang dish towels; add hooks for utensils and other essentials. Affix coat hooks to empty wall space for hanging up coats, towels, purses and backpacks.

KITCHEN CORNERS are perfect shelving opportunities for storing everything you need for the day-to-day: plates and cups and a coffeepot tucked underneath. Small freestanding wall shelves are about $10 to $30 at many home improvement centers.

IF MODULAR CABINET sizes don't exactly sync up with your available space, fill in openings with narrow pullout shelving. Get DIY drawer kits that let you customize drawer widths. Make drawer fronts to match surrounding cabinets.

GO MANUAL! Hand-operated small appliances—such as a hand mixer and a French press—are compact and don't have tangles of electrical cords (and a French press makes a great cup of coffee!). ■

THE GIANT BOOK OF TINY HOMES

Even space above door openings can be used for storage.

LOOK FOR DUAL-PURPOSE OPPORTUNITIES. A BUTCHER-BLOCK KITCHEN COUNTER CAN BE USED AS A CUTTING BOARD FOR FOOD PREP.

Sliding barn-type doors with glass panels let light flow between rooms.

43

Concrete-slab foundations won't leak and are built low to the ground, eliminating entryway stairs.

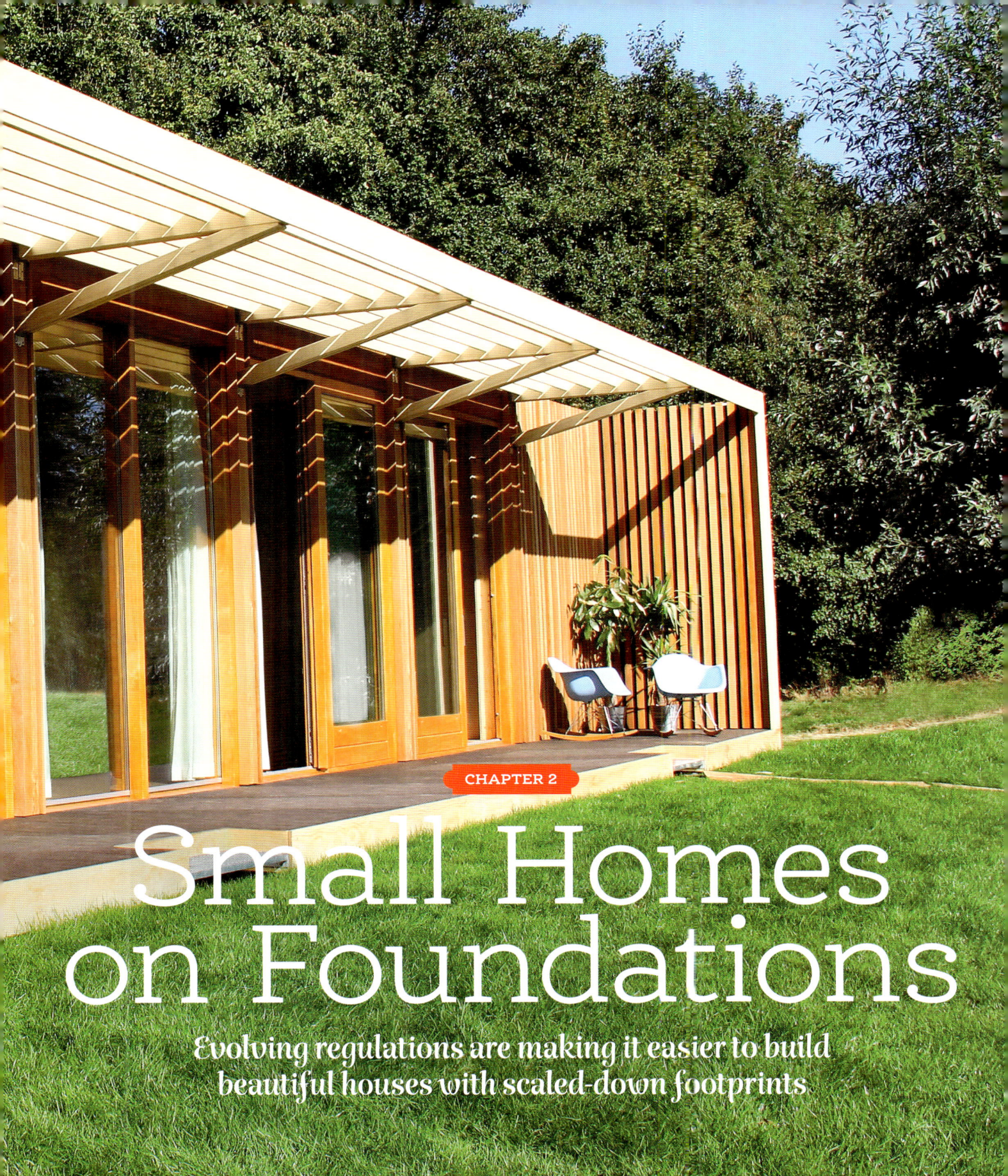

CHAPTER 2

Small Homes on Foundations

Evolving regulations are making it easier to build beautiful houses with scaled-down footprints

SMALL HOMES ON FOUNDATIONS

330 SQUARE FEET

Smaller Than Small

Smart design turns a teeny dwelling into an Asheville couple's dream palace

> SHED-STYLE ROOFS ARE SIMPLE, LOW-COST FEATURES THAT ARE EASY TO BUILD AND PRESENT A CLEAN, MODERN PROFILE.

STAYING ATTACHED
The main living area, at left, connects to a storage shed, where the couple keeps tools, hiking gear and Chad's drum set.

LISA NEYLAN AND CHAD CLAY
The couple downsized from 672 to 330 square feet.

Chad Clay and Lisa Neylan were living in a sweet, 672-square-foot 1926 bungalow when they realized their house just wasn't right. In fact, it wasn't small enough. Years before, the couple had found their little charmer and fell in love with it, virtually buying it on the spot. The bungalow came on a big lot in Asheville, North Carolina, and after about two years of living there, Chad and Lisa decided to add a rental unit at the back of the property as an income source.

Because the city required that an additional dwelling unit not be larger than 50 percent of the main house, Chad and Lisa had to come up with a secondary house no bigger than about 330 square feet. But they also had to make sure the house had at least 300 square feet of living space—at that time Asheville's legal minimum size for a two-person residence.

For help hitting that narrow target, the couple turned to Wishbone Tiny Homes, a local Asheville company that specializes in building smaller houses ranging from 200 to 2,000 square feet. The couple presented Wishbone with what Lisa describes as "a decidedly ambitious list of must-haves," including space for a king-size bed, a separate bedroom on the ground floor, sleeping space for guests, an office and enough space to stretch out and do yoga. In addition, the on-the-go couple needed storage for their bicycles, hiking gear and Chad's drum set. And don't forget special accommodations for their hound/boxer mixed-breed pal, Winston.

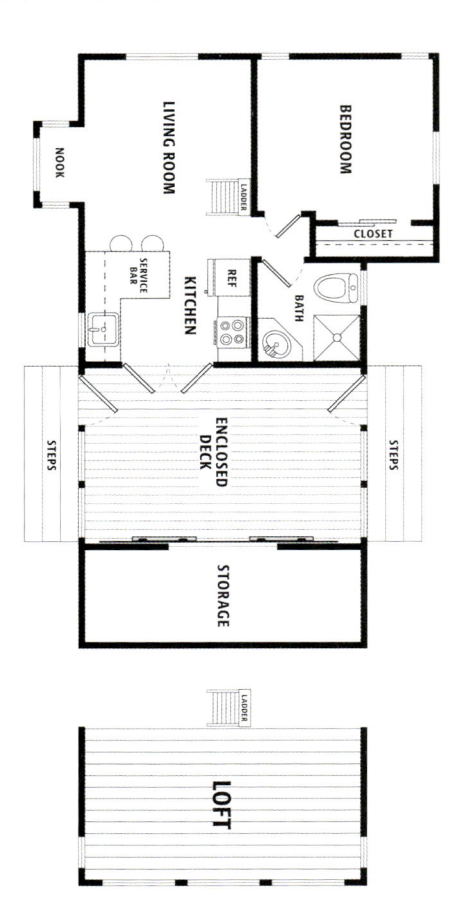

SMALL HOMES ON FOUNDATIONS

To ensure they had plenty of storage, Chad and Lisa proposed a shed connected to the house with a deck. Wishbone went a step or two better and suggested turning the deck into a 10x15-foot screened-in porch that wouldn't count against the maximum allowable square footage, with a 6x15-foot storage shed positioned on the opposite side of the porch. By connecting the shed and porch to the main house with a single roofline, the whole structure gained a cohesive, unified look and the practicality of a much larger space.

"That's what really makes the house special," says Lisa, "because that screened-in porch in this three-season environment is truly another living room."

Inside, the smallish rooms flow into one another in sensible traffic patterns. The kitchen, for example, was positioned next to the doorway to the porch so that it would be handy to the screened-in veranda.

OUTDOORS IN
The covered porch was originally an open deck. Cozy furniture and a ceiling fan turn the deck into a generous three-season living area.

49

⌂ SMALL HOMES ON FOUNDATIONS

"OUR HOUSE LIVES LARGE. IT'S BIG ENOUGH FOR US AND OUR DOG, BUT IT ONLY TAKES 40 MINUTES TO CLEAN."
—LISA NEYLAN

WALK THROUGH
Glass doors allow daylight to pour into the kitchen, and keep the food prep area close to the porch for alfresco dining.

"We originally thought to have the kitchen tucked toward the other side of the house," says Lisa, "but it made more sense to have the kitchen accessible to the outdoor area."

As the design for a cozy backyard cottage began to take shape, Chad and Lisa realized they weren't creating an ADU as much as they were building their own dream house, one which they were able to create from scratch.

"As we got started building, we realized that although the new house was smaller, because we designed it for ourselves, it made a lot more sense," says Chad. "We became attached to it and thought that we'd rather live in the new house out back than the current house out front."

"I've always been drawn to small homes and the idea of small living," Lisa says. "We've lived in apartments and even out of our Pontiac Vibe. So this house is really our dream palace." ∎

ON THE UPSIDE
The sleeping loft is accessed by ladder and creates a sheltering ceiling for the kitchen. The design opens up to a vaulted roof over the main living area.

51

🏠 SMALL HOMES ON FOUNDATIONS

400 SQUARE FEET

Greener Living
in a Small Space

The author explains why her tiny home is naturally environmentally-friendly

TRICK OF THE EYE
A bank of tall mirrors above the outdoor couch reflects light and adds a sense of depth that makes the small side yard feel more expansive.

52 THE GIANT BOOK OF TINY HOMES

I believe you can live comfortably and contentedly in—and with—a smaller footprint. And a few years after moving into my less-than-400-square-foot home, I started "The Tiny Canal Cottage" platform to prove it. (See tinycanalcottage.com for more details.)

The key to living in a small home or apartment is not figuring out how to puzzle a life's worth of stuff into limited space. It's about understanding what you truly need (and don't need) in order to live practically and happily every day.

It was nine years ago that I moved into a 1920s craftsman house in Venice Beach, California, with my rescue beagle mix and my boyfriend, Adam. We adopted a second dog, and eventually Adam and I got married on our tiny front stoop. We became business partners (working full time from our home) and before long, we welcomed our son into this unique world of ours.

We believe that small-space living will be more relevant to increasingly larger groups of people. Smaller spaces are less expensive to build, plus they may significantly reduce your environmental footprint. For example, there are fewer materials to use and transport when building a tiny home.

ADDED PLUS
A drying rack not only saves energy and space, it also saves your clothes (dryer use weakens fabric).

53

🏠 SMALL HOMES ON FOUNDATIONS

> OPTING FOR AN ARRAY OF PLANTS IS A CREATIVE WAY TO AVOID FILLING YOUR HOME WITH MASS-PRODUCED DECORATIVE OBJECTS.

ORGANIZED SPACE
Compact countertop appliances and a minimum of dishes and drinkware keep the kitchen looking clean and clutter-free.

Similarly, there are far fewer interior spaces to outfit with fixtures, appliances and furnishings. This means there are also fewer items to fix and update, all of which ultimately cuts back on production, transportation, packaging and general waste. Having fewer possessions reduces your household's overall retail consumption and the affiliated carbon footprint.

In addition, smaller homes simply use less energy than their larger counterparts. A well-insulated small space minimizes the cost required to heat, cool and illuminate. According to the U.S. Energy Information Administration, the electrical consumption of the average 2,600-square-foot American home is 914 kWh per month. Last year, our monthly electrical bills averaged about 98 kWh per month.

There are many secondary benefits of small-space living. On a daily basis, this lifestyle encourages folks to get outside and enjoy the natural world and surrounding community. That can translate to less energy being used within the home, as residents are often outdoors (requiring no utilities), or in shared local spots that are serving numerous people.

Looking for simple ways to go greener in your small space? Here are five easy ways to start.

NATURE CALLS
Plants make a bedroom a serene escape from the hectic pace of it all.

HOMEY TOUCH
Handmade items, such as the book holders on the partition wall, add charm and functionality.

ECO-FRIENDLY
Fill existing glass bottles with nontoxic homemade cleaners.

•••

"DETAILS ARE CRUCIAL IN COMPACT SPACES, WHERE EVERYTHING CATCHES THE EYE."
—WHITNEY LEIGH MORRIS

•••

🏠 SMALL HOMES ON FOUNDATIONS

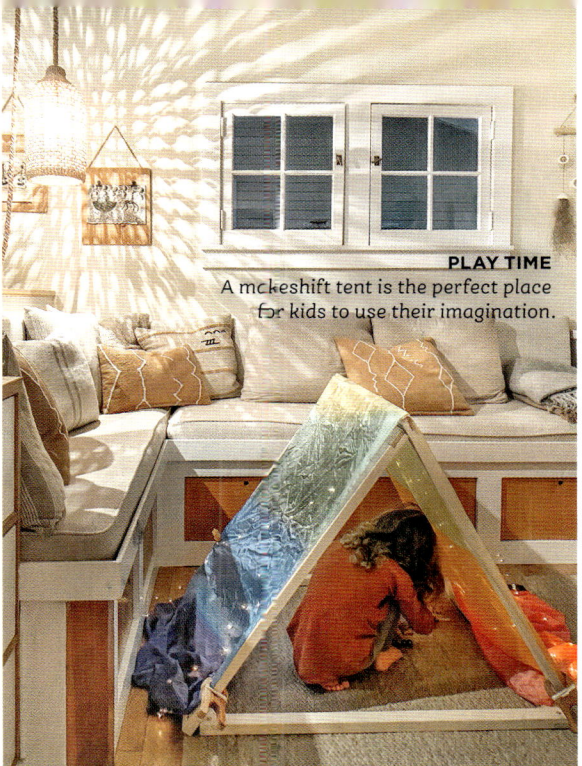

PERFECT SPOT
A crib fits in a closet-size space (left) with supplies in handy pullout storage bins.

PLAY TIME
A makeshift tent is the perfect place for kids to use their imagination.

1 | Avoid Single-Use Disposable Goods

There are lots of long-lasting, stylish alternatives to single-use goods, so try to ditch disposable items and replace them with greener alternatives. You can reduce household waste and free up storage space by transitioning from plastic razors to safety razors; from cotton balls to washable cotton rounds; from toothpaste tubes and deodorant canisters to DIY or refillable formulas; from tissues to cloth wipes; from paper towels to European dish cloths; from plastic food-storage bags to linen-and-beeswax wrap; or from Q-tips to cleanable ear swabs.

2 | Make Your Own Cleaning Supplies, or Refill Glass Bottles With Concentrates

Whether you craft your own multipurpose cleaners or refill existing bottles and jars with concentrates, you can completely cut single-use plastic out of your cleaning routine while streamlining (and beautifying) your supplies.

3 | Don't Replace Plastic With Plastic

When your existing plastic kitchenwares and various goods are worn out, replace them with stainless steel or compostable alternatives. When shopping for items like storage bins and toys, consider items made of wood, wicker and other natural materials.

SMALL HOMES ON FOUNDATIONS

4 | Rethink Your Body Products
Homemade shampoo, conditioner and shave bars often last longer than bottled supplies and produce little waste, especially if you store them in reusable glass containers. They also consume far fewer inches in a bathroom that has a tight fit. As for cosmetics, refillable palettes and multipurpose products will reduce waste and preserve space while at home and on the go, while still fulfilling your needs.

5 | Stop Buying "New"
People who live in small spaces know by necessity how important it is to stop the influx of additional items into the home. When a purchase is required, try to seek out secondhand items in lieu of newly manufactured goods. Not only will this give new life to items that are already in the waste stream, but it will also amplify the character of your space, enhancing its one-of-a-kind look and feel.

— Whitney Leigh Morris

DECORATIVE TOUCH
Repurposed pots help turn outdoor spaces into flourishing gardens full of texture and color. Gravel walkways keep dirt at bay.

JOYS OF SUMMER
An outdoor shower (above) is perfect for washing off sandy feet. Author Whitney Leigh Morris works on her home (right).

PRACTICAL & FUNCTIONAL
The built-in sofa bed (left) is perfect for a nap and overnight guests, and has storage compartments below. Kitchen scraps end up in the outdoor compost bin (below).

MULTIPURPOSE
One room serves as the family's office, living room, playroom and pop-up dining room.

SMALL HOMES ON FOUNDATIONS

HIDDEN GEM
The house is sited for maximum privacy and for ocean views. A standing-seam metal roof, PVC trim and clear cedar shingles help protect against coastal New England weather.

411 SQUARE FEET

Cottage Classic

High-end materials (and a focus on details) define this New England oceanside getaway

SMALL HOMES ON FOUNDATIONS

> A NEUTRAL COLOR SCHEME, SUCH AS THE WHITE-AND-LIGHT-GRAY USED HERE, OPENS UP SMALL SPACES AND LETS SOME DASHES OF COLOR REALLY STAND OUT.

LOOKING UP
Structural, whitewashed Douglas fir beams support a soaring cathedral ceiling. The stone fireplace and gas-burning insert give the house cozy appeal.

62 THE GIANT BOOK OF TINY HOMES

COOKING LIGHT
Instead of an oven, Beth Marcus chose a compact, countertop microwave to complement the stovetop.

DECKED OUT
Kitchen features include a Sub-Zero under-cabinet refrigerator, a two-burner Viking stove, a 16-inch dishwasher and a combo pantry and broom closet.

Although the originator of the quote, "If I had more time I would have written a shorter letter," isn't known, the meaning of the quote is apparent: It's more challenging to create something small that fulfills its purpose really well than it is to create something sprawling and incoherent—it's all about what you pack into each word. That sentiment applies to home-building, as any tiny home enthusiast knows.

When Mac Lloyd—co-owner with his wife, Lucy, of Creative Cottages LLC—designed this Freeport, Maine, oceanside retreat for homeowner Beth Marcus, he had many parameters—lot size; eco-concerns and proximity to water; setbacks; building codes—and, of course, Marcus' desires. Think of the outcome as a well-crafted haiku rather than a novel.

The 411-square-foot house—used as a getaway by Marcus, who lives full time in Virginia—is a classic colonial-style home writ small. It's not a twee dollhouse but rather a sophisticated, light-filled and comfortable home.

"The thing that draws people to this house," says Lucy Lloyd, referring to the fact that photos of the house have gone viral on social media, "is careful design in a small space."

The Lloyds do not have a tiny-house repertoire; they build homes of any size but, says Lucy, they pay careful attention to details. The challenge for a designer doing small homes is that "things can be measured in inches, not feet," Lucy says. "It's like designing a schooner. Start with everything you want and work backward. Beth told us what she wanted in the kitchen and we figured out how to fit what we could. And some things need to be multiuse."

The cottage is basically a single large area that encompasses a full kitchen, an elegant bathroom, a living room with a fireplace, a bedroom and a

63

🏠 SMALL HOMES ON FOUNDATIONS

WALL OF WINDOWS
Glass doors offer big views and flood the bedroom and sitting area with lots of light.

loft. Space-saving design details, such as tucking a stackable washer and dryer inside the bathroom and hiding the bath behind a sliding barn door, ensure that amenities aren't ignored. The TV in the bedroom area is on an arm that allows it to turn out and be enjoyed in the living room.

There's storage under the house in a crawl space and in a loft accessed by drop-down stairs.

Marcus says her goal was to have "something cozy." The design includes a cathedral ceiling, which gives the small house plenty of volume. But to bring in light and break up the roof's pitch and

> "IT'S LIKE DESIGNING A SCHOONER. START WITH EVERYTHING YOU WANT AND WORK BACKWARD."
> —LUCY LLOYD

EASY GLIDER
A sliding barn-style door to the bathroom saves lots of floor space.

make the space appear bigger, Mac Lloyd included four dormers and large oceanside windows.

Marcus loves her getaway and says she'd spend more time in the house but for the fact that she has six dogs—and only two can fit. "I love the coziness of the house; everything is right here." ∎

SMALL HOMES ON FOUNDATIONS

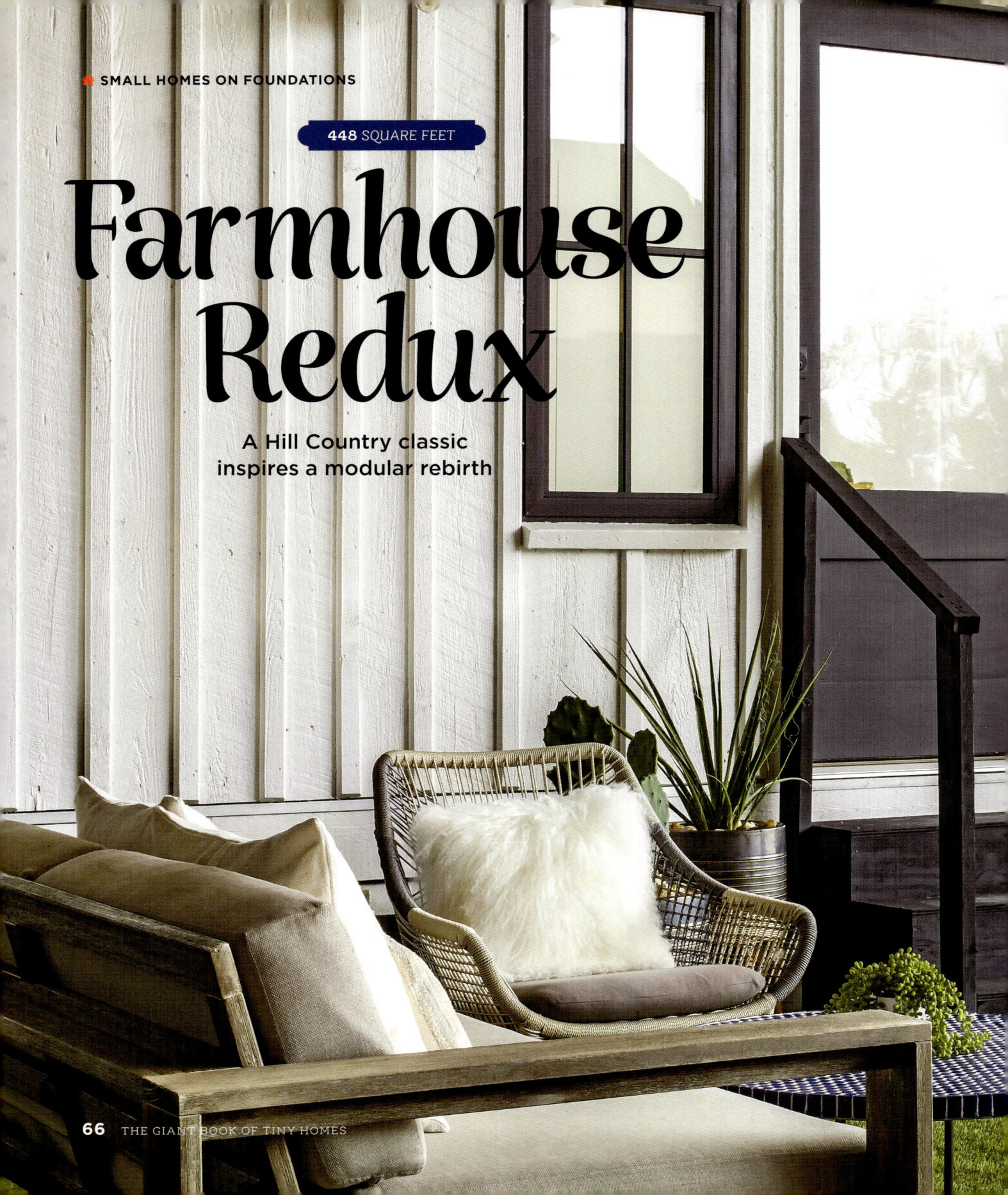

448 SQUARE FEET

Farmhouse Redux

A Hill Country classic inspires a modular rebirth

66 THE GIANT BOOK OF TINY HOMES

> DATING TO THE EARLY 1800s, AMERICAN FARMHOUSE STYLE HONORS SIMPLICITY AND STURDINESS.

BATTENED DOWN
Board-and-batten siding reclaimed from a Kentucky distillery gives state-of-the-art modular construction a timeless finish.

They're scattered across the Hill Country of central Texas—sturdy little board-and-batten farmhouses, some dating to the early 1800s. Characterized by sleeping lofts tucked under high gables and tall windows built for ventilation, the model packed a lot of function into a small footprint. Those strengths, along with the style's rugged good looks, convinced Austin-based modular home builder Tracen Gardner that it was high time for a farmhouse revival.

"The simple farmhouse design has stood the test of time," Gardner explains. "It has been used for many years, withstood many storms and almost two centuries of building styles." Gardner knows the style intimately. His company, Reclaimed Space, incorporates recycled materials into its modular homes. Those materials often come from farmhouses too far gone to rehab. What could be better than a revived farmhouse built with the same solid lumber?

The result is a 14-by-32-foot home that uses the farmhouse's signature gable roof to provide loft sleeping space for four. The ground floor has a bedroom, dining/living area, bathroom and a kitchen with full-size appliances—all in 448 square feet.

The style appealed to Kent and Melissa Ferguson, although when they first learned of Gardner's project they had some reservations about the concept. "We heard the word 'modular' and weren't particularly interested," Kent recalls. But once they visited a prototype Reclaimed Space was constructing, they quickly changed their minds. "We really liked the way it captured the vintage character of a Hill Country farmhouse." They commissioned a slightly enlarged version as a weekend retreat. Gardner's team built it in a mere 45 days.

• • •

EVEN THE COTTON INSULATION IS RECYCLED, USING COWBOY-APPROPRIATE DENIM SCRAPS AND CLIPPINGS.

• • •

67

SMALL HOMES ON FOUNDATIONS

How was that possible? "Our homes are one-hundred-percent shop-built," Gardner explains. That means construction is out of the weather, with all the tools and materials close at hand. "When the house ships out on an 18-wheeler, everything is done—floors finished, toilet paper holders in place, cabinets, ceiling fans—everything." In contrast to the six to nine months it takes to build a home on site, Reclaimed Space can complete a modular unit in five to eight weeks. "And they'll be better constructed than a site-built home," Gardner maintains.

Although framed with conventional materials, Gardner used reclaimed lumber inside and out. Kent jokes about the contrasting provenance of the reclaimed lumber: "The siding may be from an 1830s Kentucky bourbon distillery but the flooring is from a Texas church. So we feel they offset each other." Even the cotton insulation is recycled, using cowboy-appropriate denim scraps and clippings.

PARTING WAYS
A partition wall separates the living room from the master bedroom. Keeping things light makes the space feel larger.

OPEN AIR
Wood shelving offers a farmhouse feel and is a great alternative to the heavy look of over-counter upper cabinets.

MODERN CONVENIENCES WRAPPED IN HISTORIC MATERIALS OFFER THE BEST OF BOTH WORLDS.

NEW LIFE
The repurposed beadboard ceiling was clear-coated to stabilize the shabby-chic alligatored paint. Tall, narrow windows are a farmhouse hallmark.

🏠 SMALL HOMES ON FOUNDATIONS

SLEEPOVER
The loft has 4½ feet of headroom and can accommodate four sleeping bags and air mattresses— a great nesting area for kids.

The house was transported to its site, but it wasn't built on a trailer bed like most tiny homes. "Our reclaimed materials are not light," Gardner says. "The cypress and oak we use can be three to eight times heavier than new rough-sawn cedar." The dense, well-seasoned old–growth lumber is tough stuff. "We go through a lot of saw blades," Gardner explains, smiling. "We can't even pound a nail into a lot of that wood. We have to drill first, then use special construction screws." Other drawbacks lurk in the shabby-chic look of the lumber: Old paint can harbor things you don't want—like lead. That called for stabilizing the ceiling beadboard with a clear coat of polyurethane.

The finished house—perched above the Pedernales River on a remote site where aoudad sheep and wild turkey wander by—has exceeded Kent and Melissa's expectations. "We love the simplicity," says Kent. "If you have more space, you just fill it with more stuff." ■

ROOM TO SPARE
Sleeping areas include a master bedroom with a queen bed, plus the loft and a sofa bed. In a pinch, guests can even sleep on the porch.

NO PRIMITIVE PRIVY
The modular home has a full bath equipped with a tub/shower and full-size vanity, and tile flooring inspired by a "Wild Geese" country quilt.

The Cost of Reclaimed

In the 1920s, the Aladdin kit home company offered a dollar for every knot found in its lumber—a testament to the clear, knot-free old-growth lumber available back then. Much of that great old lumber still exists, waiting to be reclaimed. But harvesting it from old structures calls for intensive labor and ingenious methods. Gardner and his team have developed special prying tools for pulling off old lumber and use some unusual prep techniques. "Sometimes we take off the roof and wait for rain," Gardner says with a laugh. Soaking the wood reduces splitting. All nails must be removed and any splits and cracks sawn off.

SMALL HOMES ON FOUNDATIONS

NORTHERN EXPOSURE
A jaunty, hipped roof, exposed rafter tails and a shingled exterior give Lorraine's house a regional, Northwest flavor.

664 SQUARE FEET

Sweet Dreaming

Lorraine Olsen didn't just build a house—she imagined it

SMALL HOMES ON FOUNDATIONS

It was a canyon. Not a big, yawning opening, but a steep and narrow fissure where a humble creek burbled down, cleaving its way through the town of Ashland, Oregon. Lorraine Olsen brought her dog and sat on the slope and watched the pines and alders and cottonwoods sway in the gentle, ever-present canyon breeze. And she imagined a house.

"It's all so beautiful and peaceful," she says of the smallish, undeveloped lot that she'd bought and then proceeded to contemplate for nearly three years. "I'd come with the dog and sit there and meditate on the house I wanted to build."

It wouldn't be the first time the Oregon native had thought about a house.

COOLING OFF
Breezes that flow along the ravine and the walk-out design help stabilize interior temps and makes air conditioning unnecessary.

"My whole life I've had house dreams," says Lorraine. "I've been having them since I was a teenager. They always were fantastical houses with secret passageways and hidden places, and in the dreams I was always looking for a house."

But as dreamy as her lot may have been, it was a problematic piece of ground, constrained by a floodplain, a steep grade, a utility easement, lot line setbacks and the city's solar restrictions, which limit the height of a structure.

To help make her dreams a reality, Lorraine turned to local architect Carlos Delgado.

"The allowable footprint was much smaller than anyone had anticipated," Delgado says.

74 THE GIANT BOOK OF TINY HOMES

LOTS OF GLASS WITH VIEWS TO THE OUTSIDE HELPS THE INTERIORS OF SMALL HOMES FEEL LARGER.

DO THE BUMP
A bump-out makes a cozy window seat in the living room.

"That's common—people look at a lot and see a lot of space, but the actual buildable area is restricted."

Putting their heads together, the homeowner and the architect came up with a two-story structure with a modest footprint that nestles into the lot. With its 357-square-foot footprint and 664 total square feet, the house is about as big as it can be and still comply with all the limitations imposed by the steep lot.

"I was absolutely confident about what I wanted when we started designing," Lorraine says. "After all, I'd been thinking about this house, like, forever. Carlos and his team were so supportive of my ideas."

75

▲ SMALL HOMES ON FOUNDATIONS

SET BACK
Located in a ravine, the two-story house is nearly hidden from passersby, its roof almost even with street level.

Lorraine's vision put the single bedroom on the upper floor and the kitchen and the living room on the lower walk-out level. That called for some designing legerdemain at the entryway, where the main entry door, the door to the bedroom, a laundry closet and the stairwell all converged.

"The biggest challenge with a small two-story house usually is the staircase," Delgado says. "It eats up so much interior square footage."

Delgado's solution was a welcoming, light-filled stairwell that encourages visitors to follow it down to the main living area, and he deflected attention from the bedroom door by setting it at an oblique angle. Instead of a solid wall that followed the staircase downward on its interior side, Delgado pushed the bedroom wall back slightly, opening up a channel for light from the exterior stairwell windows to penetrate down alongside the staircase and into the living area.

To keep as much "stuff" out of the building envelope as possible and maximize living space, the house has no HVAC system or ductwork.

SPRINGTIME BOUQUET
Homeowner Lorraine arranges flowers in her kitchen.

Instead, the building relies on thick insulation in its 2x6 walls and the fact that it is nestled into the hillside, where the relatively constant earth temps help mitigate interior temperature fluctuations. A small gas heater provides all the warmth that's needed in winter, and cooling air that flows down the canyon makes mechanical air-conditioning unnecessary in summer.

"The thing I like best about this house is its location," says Lorraine. "I love the breezes in the summer and how it's tucked into this little green glade. I'd like this house if it was somewhere else, but here I see gorgeous beauty out of every window. I just feel so appreciative and fortunate."

Although Lorraine says she used to think of a 1,000-square-foot house as "small," today she embraces the compact proportions that make up her dream house.

"It feels like the right size for one person," she says. "I know everyone is different, but I like the idea of not having space I'm not using. It feels more comfortable to me. It's the right size for me. After all, I dreamed this house into existence!" ∎

What's Solar Access?

Many cities restrict the height of buildings and sometimes trees so neighbors have access to plenty of sunshine to warm their houses in cool weather and power solar-energy systems. The Oregon Department of Energy calculates that buildings that get full sunshine may use 20 percent less energy than those with limited sunlight. In Ashland, Oregon, structures may not cast a shadow across the northern property line that's greater than would be cast by a 6-foot-high fence at 12 p.m. on December 21.

SURROUNDED BY NATURE
Windows on three sides of the bedroom allow daylight and fresh air to wash inside.

SMALL HOMES ON FOUNDATIONS

743 SQUARE FEET

Way Outside the Box

A customized, prefabricated cabin connects with the landscape and makes small live large

RURAL LOCATIONS MAY HAVE UNIQUE BUILDING CODES. BE SURE TO CHECK WITH COUNTY AUTHORITIES FOR REGULATIONS.

When people hear the term "prefab home," they might think of a house that's cheaply built and devoid of character.

Au contraire! You only have to look at the New Hampshire prefab house of Alex Grossman and David Park to dispel those notions. Built as a summer getaway, the 743-square-foot cabin features gorgeous timber frame construction and exquisite details. Exposed beams, natural wood paneling and finely crafted hardware and fixtures bring this prefab house into the realm of architectural excellence.

What's more, the Grossman/Park house benefited from one of the best attributes of prefab construction—the exterior shell came together in less than two weeks. The speedy process of prefab construction helps lessen the chance that the building crew might encounter weather delays, and it also helps keep labor costs in check.

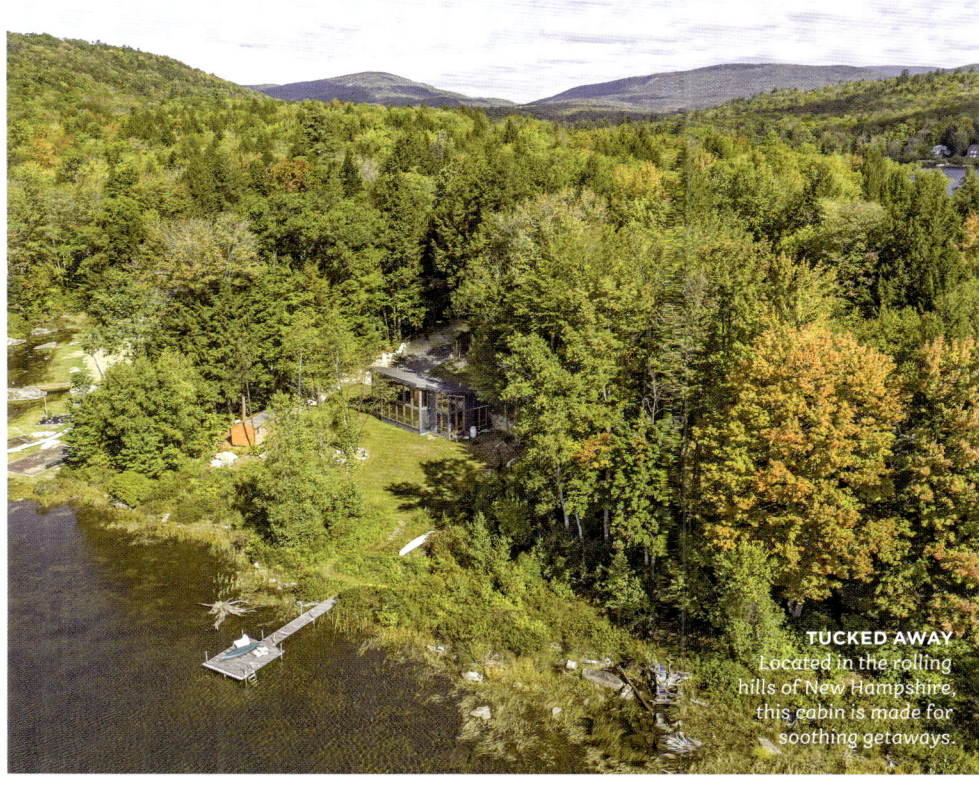

TUCKED AWAY
Located in the rolling hills of New Hampshire, this cabin is made for soothing getaways.

79

🏠 SMALL HOMES ON FOUNDATIONS

"Any house component that gets precut at a factory and assembled on site is considered prefab," explains Emory Baldwin, principal architect and founder of FabCab, based in Seattle. "On this house we used a timber frame and SIP [structurally insulated panel] combination."

FabCab works with mills on both the West and East Coasts. In this case, the company worked with its East Coast partner, who used a CNC (computer numerical control) machine to cut Douglas fir logs to FabCab's specifications. The pieces, along with the proper screws and dowels, are then numbered and barcoded, shrink-wrapped, placed on pallets in a logical order and shipped

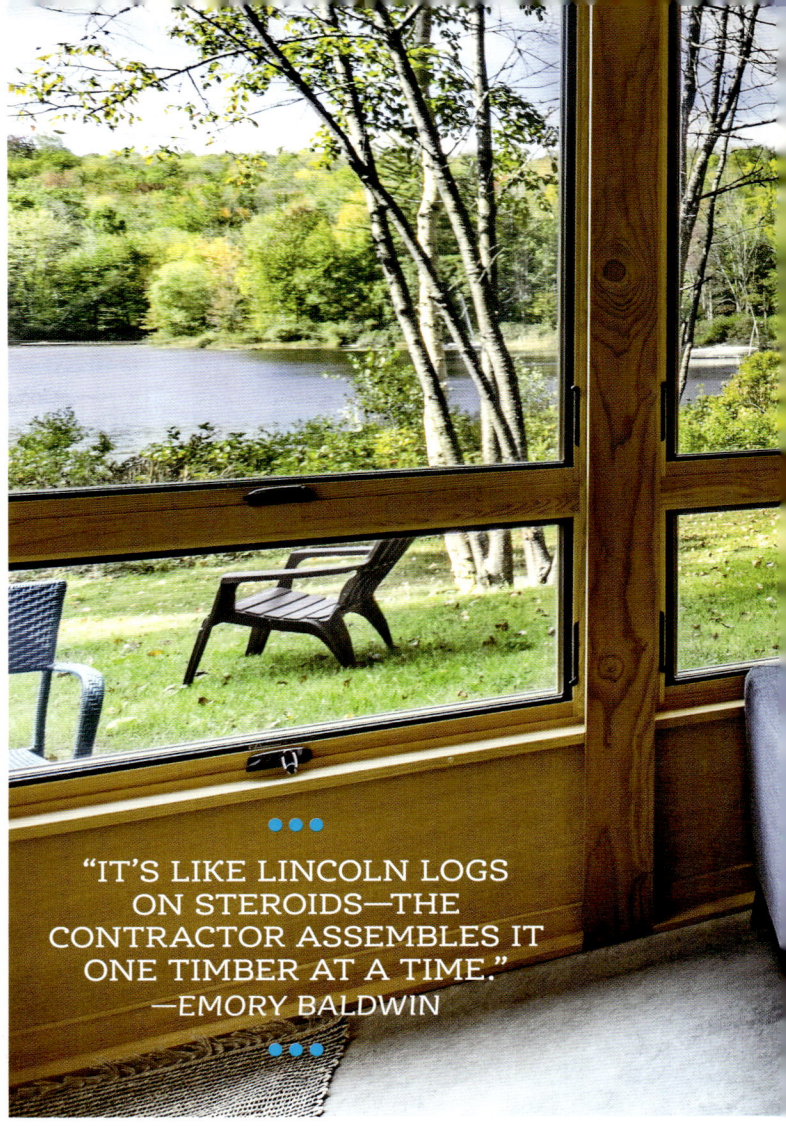

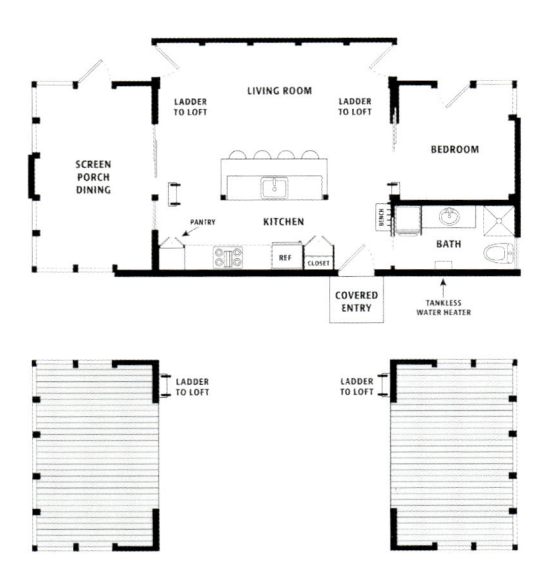

LOFTY AIRS
A 14-foot-high ceiling allows for a loft sleeping space on each end of the house.

"IT'S LIKE LINCOLN LOGS ON STEROIDS—THE CONTRACTOR ASSEMBLES IT ONE TIMBER AT A TIME."
—EMORY BALDWIN

80 THE GIANT BOOK OF TINY HOMES

PERFECT FIT
The pond and the landscape become part of the interior with a wall of windows.

SMOOTH TRANSITION
Clear wood paneling and polished concrete floors give the cabin a contemporary look that extends to the screened porch.

by truck to the site. The builder has access to screenshots of 3D models to show how it should be assembled.

"It's like Lincoln Logs on steroids," Baldwin says. "The contractor assembles it one timber at a time in a traditional timber frame method."

Once the timber frame is up, the premade wall panels arrive on site. For walls, FabCab uses SIP panel construction. An SIP has a thick, insulating foam core laminated between two pieces of oriented strand board. The result is a rigid, lightweight, inert panel that can be cut out for windows and doors and still maintain structural integrity. SIPs do away with the need for traditional stud framing and added insulation.

"There are very few gaps with an SIPs home," Baldwin says. "This house is tight and energy efficient." To get fresh air into the cabin, FabCab

SMALL HOMES ON FOUNDATIONS

specified a whole-house fan; for a larger home, Baldwin would choose either an HRV (heat recovery ventilator) or ERV (energy recovery ventilator) to efficiently bring in outdoor air, he says.

The cabin sits on a cement slab to which it's attached with metal "hold downs." Coming from Washington State, FabCab is attuned to the need for keeping a house connected to the ground during a wind storm or possible earthquake, Baldwin says.

Alex and David discovered FabCab after they'd lost out on the purchase of a traditional stick-built cabin—"a falling-down hunting camp with no bathroom," Grossman says.

Fortunately, they found a blank slate—an empty plot of land located on a 400-acre pond. "It's really a lake, but the State of New Hampshire calls it a pond," notes Alex. They met with an architect thinking they would build a cabin, but the encounter didn't click. "It didn't feel inspiring or fun," she recalls. "Then I saw FabCab's pictures

> MONOLITHIC CONCRETE SLABS WORK AS BOTH A FOUNDATION AND TOUGH, STAIN-RESISTANT INTERIOR FLOORING.

ISLAND APPEAL
The central island adds a dash of color that contrasts with the natural wood interiors. Sky-blue stools are fun exclamation points.

82 THE GIANT BOOK OF TINY HOMES

GOING TO WORK
Kitchen counters are a quartz composite, which is scratch- and stain-resistant. The upper bar on the island and the cabinets are beechwood.

🏠 SMALL HOMES ON FOUNDATIONS

A Prefabulous Building Method

Sheri Koones, author of several books about prefab homes (including *Prefabulous Small Houses*; 2016), says she's "worked hard over the years to help people see the reality of what prefab can look like. They are indistinguishable from site-built houses." Prefab is an umbrella term for structures with various components—walls, floors, roofs—that have been built in a controlled factory environment, then shipped and assembled on the work site. The amount of completion on prefab homes varies: Some are an empty box, others have appliances, flooring and everything else included.

online and said, '*That's* what I want.' There's nothing like this here."

The couple and their two children live full time in a circa-1700s farmhouse about nine miles away. Their cabin is a summer place from which they can still commute to their jobs. With its 14-foot ceiling, tucked-away loft bedrooms and tons of storage space, the open-floor-plan house lives large.

At the cabin, they spend much of their time outside hiking, biking, kayaking, canoeing and paddleboarding. The house is just the right size, Alex says. "It's comfortable and nice rather than having something bigger that we need to maintain."

She loves the cabin's distinctly modern feel. "It's simple and stress-free, and because it's not fussy, it feels luxurious. It allows us to have the feeling of being far away, since it's so different from our main house. We feel lucky to have this place that's so beautiful and functional." ∎

HIDDEN APPEAL
The master bedroom is located behind sliding barn doors. Above it is one of the sleeping lofts, accessible by a ship-type ladder.

ON HIGH
To prevent having to modify the exterior and to include as much glass as possible, the floor in the sleeping lofts had to be thin. Both lofts have engineered wood floors.

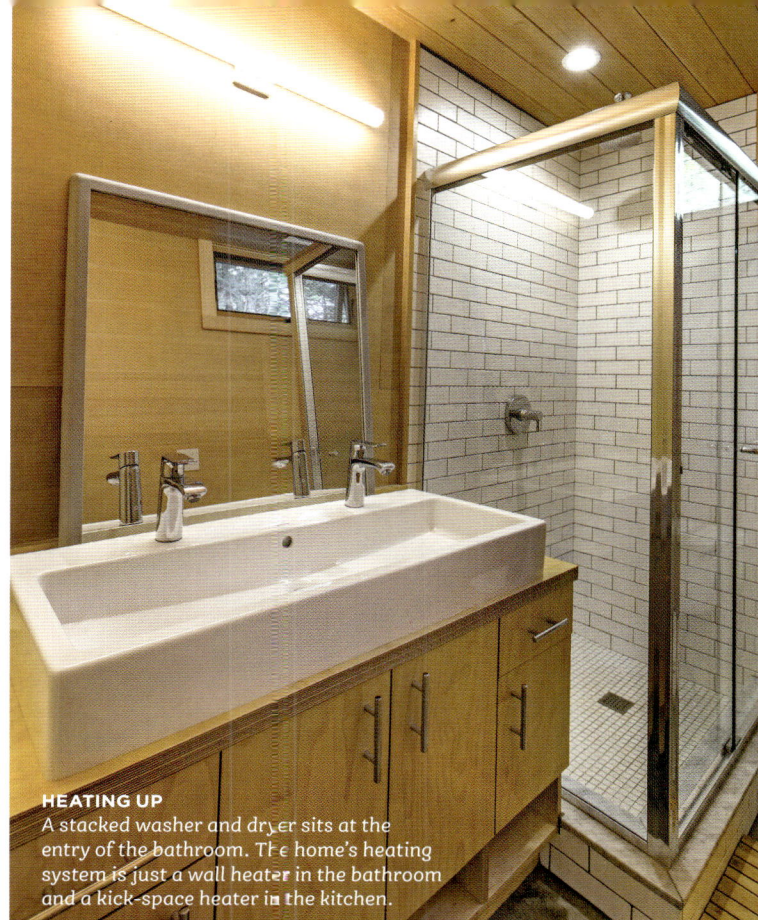

HEATING UP
A stacked washer and dryer sits at the entry of the bathroom. The home's heating system is just a wall heater in the bathroom and a kick-space heater in the kitchen.

SCREENED OFF
Simple wooden screens create a visual break between the sleeping lofts and the main living area.

85

🏠 SMALL HOMES ON FOUNDATIONS

900 SQUARE FEET

Saving Face

A California designer with a passion for older homes restores the seaside mojo of a 1940s cottage in Laguna Beach

LOW PROFILE
A low fence with classic detailing is in keeping with the scale of the house.

> SIMPLE DETAILS, SUCH AS DIVIDED-LIGHT WINDOWS AND FLOWER BOXES, HELP GIVE SMALL HOUSES CHARACTER.

Clark Collins has one word to sum up the little cottage he found for sale in Laguna Beach, California: "deplorable."

"It was in really rough shape," he adds. Fortunately for the 900-square-foot house, it had been discovered by Collins, a talented designer with an optimistic spirit.

"I've always had a passion for older homes—and especially for smaller homes with a lot of charm and a lot of character," says Collins, whose design/build firm, Collins Design & Development, specializes in remodeling the historic houses that populate the coastal-area resort towns of Southern California. Many of these houses were built from 1900 through 1950 as summer getaway homes for people from Los Angeles who came to escape the heat and congestion of the big city.

This particular cottage had been built in 1946 but had fallen into disrepair over the past many decades. Collins, however, saw it as a blank canvas that needed some respectful TLC. He bought the house with the idea of teasing out its original allure.

To do that, he researched the era for period fixtures, materials and details that matched the little house's engaging personality. Old fiberboard paneling in the living room, for instance, was

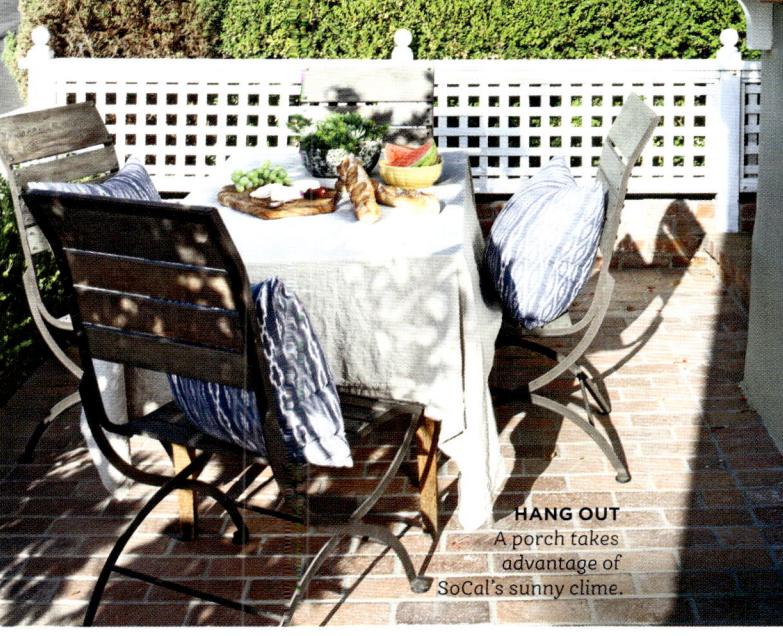

HANG OUT
A porch takes advantage of SoCal's sunny clime.

87

🏠 SMALL HOMES ON FOUNDATIONS

LIGHTING UP
A sunny eating nook makes the small galley kitchen feel luxuriously large.

OLDER HOUSES OFTEN HAVE HIDDEN TREASURES, SUCH AS CLASSIC WOOD FLOORS BURIED UNDER LAYERS OF CARPET.

replaced with tongue-and-groove board paneling that was commonly used in inexpensive 1940s bungalows. Worn carpeting was ripped up to reveal the original oak-strip flooring, which Collins promptly had refinished. Vintage light fixtures helped restore authenticity, as did ceramic light switches that were refurbished to modern codes. Even the new kitchen cabinets were outfitted with brass hinges from the 1930s.

Although all systems and appliances were thoroughly modernized to meet today's living standards, existing period touches were carefully preserved whenever practical. The single-pane windows, with their wavy glass panes, are all original, as are the built-in curio cabinets.

"The real challenge with these tiny Laguna houses is maximizing your storage space," says Collins. "Closets tend to be really small, so any little niche that we could find we'd turn into some kind of storage area. We'd add storage under stairwells, for example, and in the kitchen, we'd

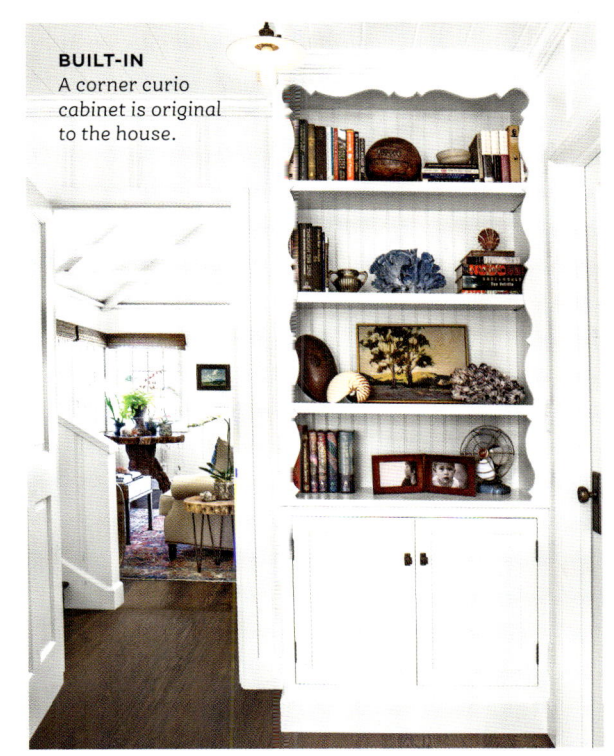

BUILT-IN
A corner curio cabinet is original to the house.

WHITE-ON-WHITE
Light tones keep the kitchen bright and upbeat. Dark soapstone counters are elegant and period-correct.

🏠 SMALL HOMES ON FOUNDATIONS

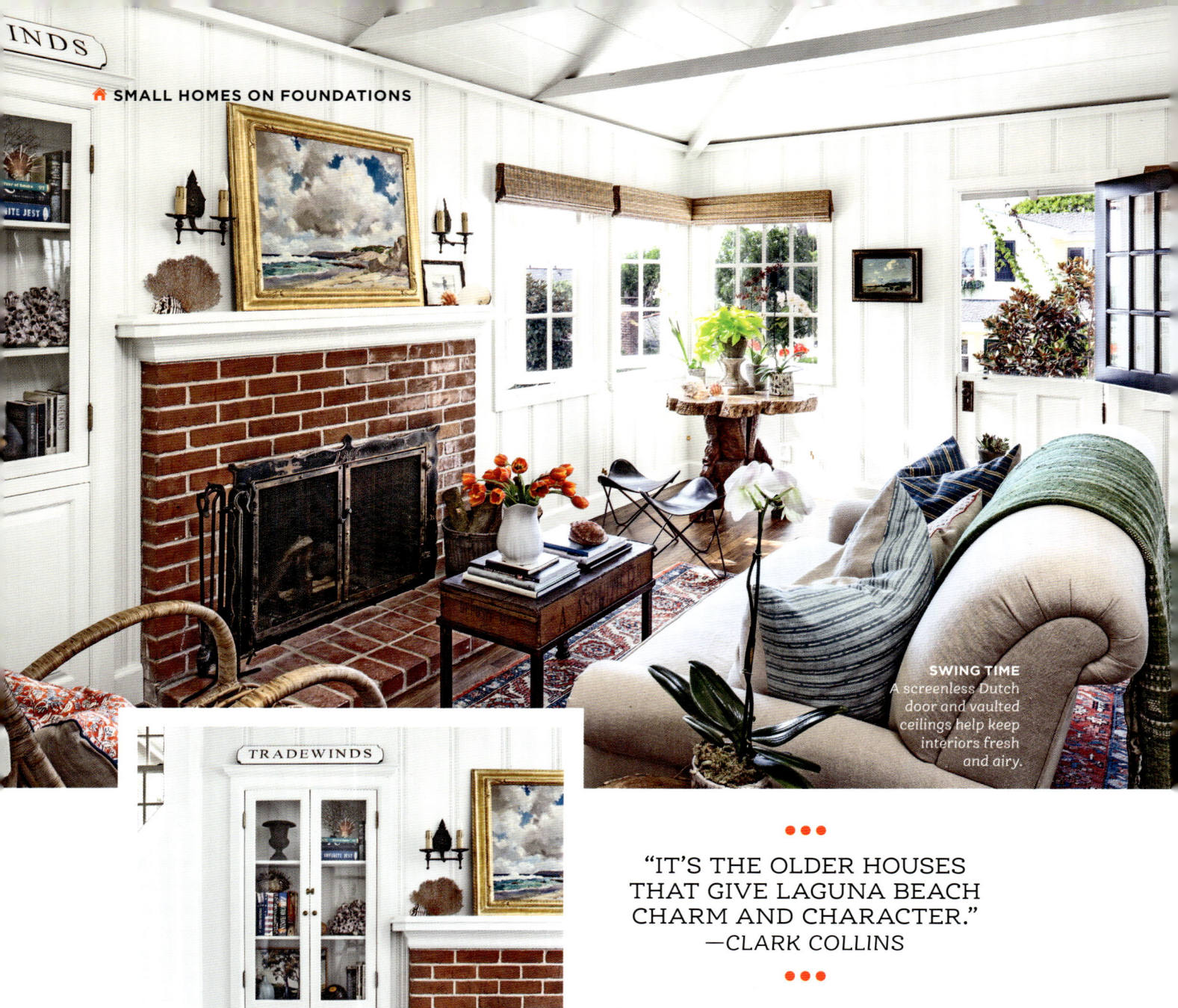

SWING TIME
A screenless Dutch door and vaulted ceilings help keep interiors fresh and airy.

•••
"IT'S THE OLDER HOUSES THAT GIVE LAGUNA BEACH CHARM AND CHARACTER."
—CLARK COLLINS
•••

replace older cabinets with uppers that go all the way to the ceiling."

As the chair of the Laguna Beach Heritage Committee, Collins is especially sensitive to development that threatens to replace the city's older housing stock with newer, larger and often less-winsome houses.

"Historic preservation in this day and age is challenging," says Collins. "Not everyone wants to preserve older houses. But these are the types of homes that give the town its character, and make it unique and desirable." ■

VINTAGE LOOK
Classic fixtures and subway tile wainscoting are both modern and retro.

CUSTOM DETAIL
When the original wall paneling couldn't be salvaged, Collins reproduced the look with custom-milled boards.

STEP OUTSIDE
The master bedroom comes complete with a private balcony that's big enough for sitting and enjoying the view.

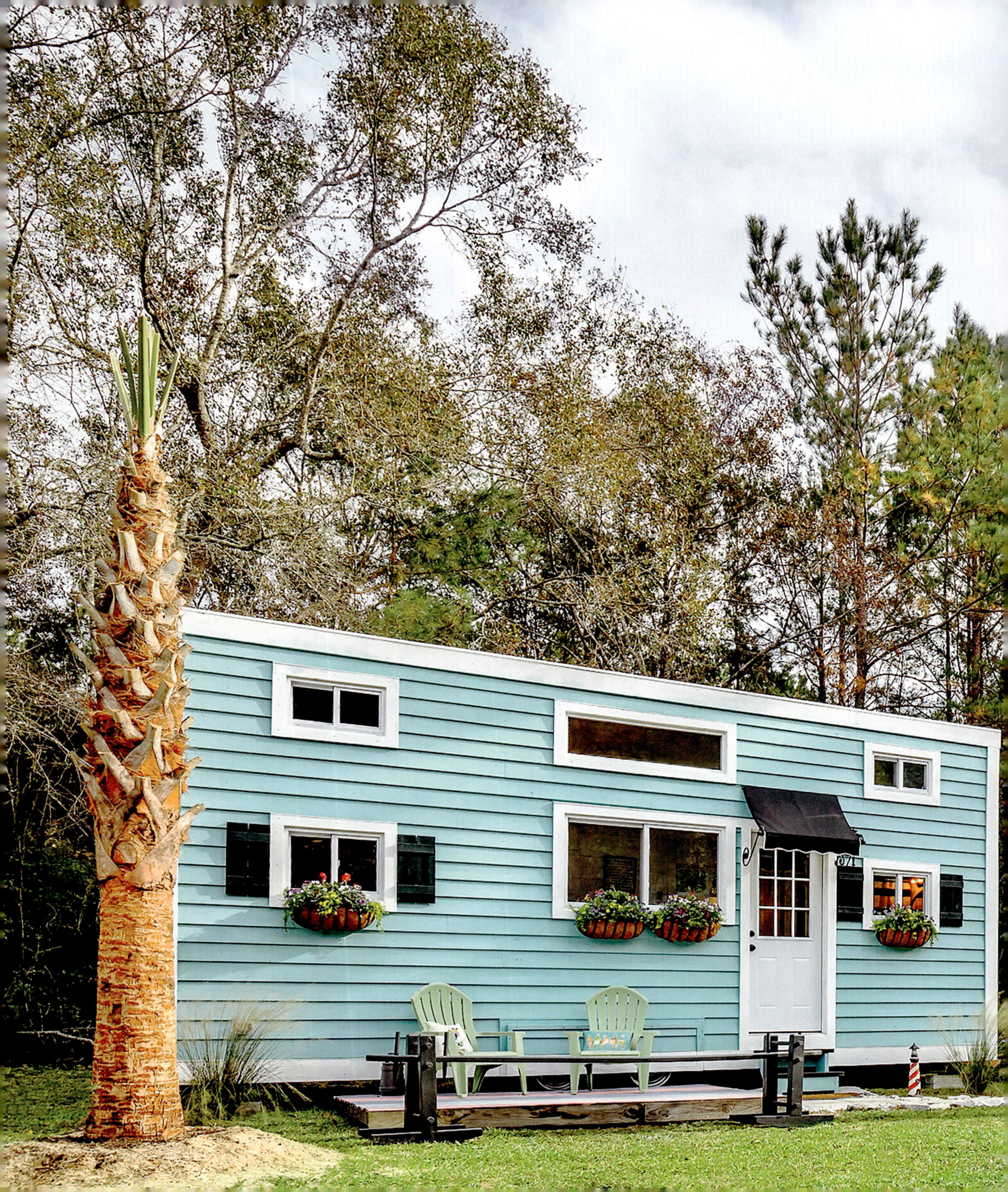

UP AND AWAY
Tiny homes are often built on trailer platforms to make them easier to move.

CHAPTER 3

Going Mobile

Indulge your wanderlust with portable tiny houses that offer all the comforts of home

GOING MOBILE

147 SQUARE FEET

Super-Small Me

A chance meeting leads to a tiny house that's a model of efficiency and clever design

TOYBOX TINY HOME
The exterior features a thermoplastic roof, colorful corrugated fiberglass panels and natural cedar-lap siding.

IT'S A SMALL, SIMPLE, MODERN, ECOLOGICALLY RESPONSIBLE, AFFORDABLE HOME THAT HELPS DEFINE AN ALTERNATIVE STANDARD OF LIVING.

GOING MOBILE

When it comes to downsizing, it would be hard to get more reduced than the Toybox Tiny Home. With a mere 147 square feet of living space, the Toybox Tiny is the inspirational grail of living small. But that doesn't mean sacrifice. This tiny house has an abundance of clever functionality, storage and livability. Plus, it's cute!

"I grew up in a household with 11 kids," says Paul Schultz, a Chicago designer with a predisposition toward designing efficient, compact, sustainable spaces. "With that many siblings, you're going to bump elbows. That's probably where I got my urge to design for efficiency."

The Toybox Tiny is the result of a chance meeting between Schultz and music student Frank Henderson. When the two met, Henderson had just purchased a trailer so he could build his own tiny house on wheels to serve as a temporary residence while he finished school. Together, they stirred up a perfect storm of tiny house-ness with the goal of creating a place of "peace, simplicity, happiness and recreation."

They sought the advice of structural engineers, carpenters, RV specialists, insulation contractors and other experts. Included in the mix were serious "doubters"—those who were convinced that such small quarters would never be livable.

HIDDEN GEMS
Kitchen cabinets were almost completely replaced by a storage wall and a spice rack above the sink that doubles as a shelf.

FEATURING A FEW KEEPSAKES PER SEASON ALLOWS FOR SENTIMENTAL ITEMS TO BE CELEBRATED WITHOUT OVERCROWDING THE SPACE.

Movable fabric-covered seating cubes have secret lives as storage bins.

GOING MOBILE

> ## Downsize & Upgrade Strategies
>
> • **Rethink** Make lists of household items:
> **1** Essentials are objects that are absolutely required for daily and weekly living.
> **2** Nonessentials are objects that are not required but may add character or appeal.
> **3** Shared items can be used by friends, family and neighbors.
>
> • **Multipurpose** Can a knife be a potato peeler? Choose objects with multiple functions. Look for furnishings that double as storage and/or have several uses.
>
> • **Let Go** Remove duplicated items. For example, a mop and a broom might be able to share the same handle. Also, consider taking a picture of a sentimental item. Sell or give away items that are truly superfluous.
>
> • **Share** Uncover ways that essential and nonessential everyday household items can be shared. For example, a set of eight place settings isn't needed every day but can be borrowed when there's a party.
>
> • **Categorize** Group essential items and determine where they can be stored. For example, in the Toybox Tiny Home, the kitchen appliances, including the stovetop, are plug-in models and can be stowed when not in use.

DUAL PURPOSE
A dining desk folds up and out of the way when not in use.

"The most informative discoveries came from conversations with people who had never considered that they could live in a home under 200 square feet," Schultz says. "By the time the prototype was complete, many of the doubters had changed their tone from 'I could never...' to 'I may be able to...' and even 'I want to downsize.' Inspiring the doubters is key to the tiny home movement succeeding and expanding so people can live in ecologically responsible homes." ■

STRAIGHT UP
A pine ship ladder is stored near the front door and becomes a room divider between the dining desk and living area.

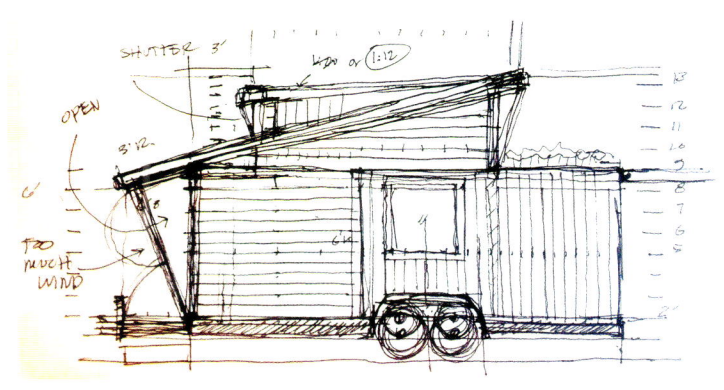

"INSPIRING THE DOUBTERS IS KEY TO THE TINY HOME MOVEMENT."
—PAUL SCHULTZ

BRIGHT IDEA
Primary colors define the Toybox Tiny Home house as playful, whimsical and fun.

GOING MOBILE

ON THE ROAD
Jenna's tiny house motors among the majestic mountains of Alaska.

165 SQUARE FEET

Giant Journey

A 25,000-mile excursion balances adventure with a love of home

> INVEST IN A GOOD GPS NAVIGATION SYSTEM. EVEN IF YOU'RE A SEAT-OF-THE-PANTS EXPLORER, IT'S THERE IF YOU NEED IT.

The porch post is a branch from a redwood tree found on Jenna's road trip.

🏠 GOING MOBILE

RUSTIC ACCENTS
Reclaimed barnwood and antique fruit crates that form a stairway to the loft offer visual appeal.

Good dog! Jenna's Australian shepherd, Salies, also hopped aboard for the road trip of a lifetime.

102 THE GIANT BOOK OF TINY HOMES

I spent one year traveling through the U.S. and Canada with my 165-square-foot tiny house. My wheels covered 25,000 miles, traveled below sea level in Death Valley National Park, over the Rocky Mountains and even through the ocean when I loaded my home onto a ferry.

My favorite memory from my tiny house travels happened during my time in Alaska. It was the summer of 2015, and I decided to tow my house to the Arctic Circle. Why? Mostly just to say I did it. The highway leading north is notoriously rough, and many RVers don't ever dare to make the trip. I knew I was risking a breakdown or (at the very least) a few flat tires. Still, I wanted to make that trip.

We took it slow. Really slow. In fact, I would say we crept our way north! Finally, after an entire day of driving, I saw a sign that read "Welcome to the Arctic Circle." Shockingly, my house made the bumpy trip with all four tires intact. I had already fixed two flat tires that month, so this was an incredible accomplishment.

I got out of the truck and jumped for joy! We made it! It was midnight, but the sun had not yet set. It was a euphoric moment.

Contrary to popular belief, traveling with a tiny house is not a cheap lifestyle. Unlike RVs, tiny houses are built using 2x4 framing, insulation and cathedral ceilings. This type of construction is heavy and, therefore, expensive to tow. My adventure came at a steep price. I towed my

•••
"TRAVELING WITH A TINY HOUSE IS NOT A CHEAP LIFESTYLE."
—JENNA SPESARD
•••

SPREAD OUT
The loft is big enough for a king-size bed, but Jenna chose a queen so she'd have room for baskets and books.

GOING MOBILE

How to Change a Flat Tire

First things first: Before you take off on your journey, ask your trailer manufacturer for the recommended torque and nut-tightening sequence for your trailer wheels, and keep that information with you at all times!

1 Loosen the lug nuts while the wheel is still on the ground.
2 Lift the tiny house using a trailer jack (the Andersen Rapid Jack is a good one), just enough that the wheel with the flat is hovering.
3 Replace the flat with the good spare.
4 Tighten the lug nuts as much as you can by hand, wiggling the new wheel in place.
5 Lower the trailer back to the ground and tighten the lug nuts to the appropriate torque and sequence.
6 Drive 20 miles, then re-torque the lug nuts to the correct specification.

10,100-pound home with a Ford F-250 diesel truck. On average I got about 9 mpg and spent $700 a month on gas! When you also factor in campground fees and other utilities, my monthly cost of living was comparable to my lifestyle prior to going tiny, when I lived in a large apartment in Los Angeles.

If you're interested in traveling with a tiny house, consider your total weight and the weight distribution during the design phase. Build with lightweight materials, otherwise you will spend more on gas, a larger truck or both. I also recommend that you purchase an anti-sway bar, GPS navigation and levelers that can handle the total weight.

Living small means something different to every "tiny houser." For me, it has always been about balancing a life of adventure with a sense of home. My tiny home has allowed me to live nomadically, in a space that I was able to customize to my own taste and personality. I feel a special connection to my tiny home, and that, to me, is priceless.

—Jenna Spesard

Flat tires are inevitable—keep a trailer jack handy!

WHAT'S IN STORE
The gable end of the storage loft features a sunburst design of reclaimed wood set around a window frame made from a tree trunk.

105

🏠 GOING MOBILE

MAKING TRACKS
Jenna and her tiny house traveled for a year throughout the U.S. and Canada. Here they are in Nova Scotia.

Peggy's Point is an iconic lighthouse in Nova Scotia.

106 THE GIANT BOOK OF TINY HOMES

> "ALLOWING EMPTY SPACE IN MY LIFE IS A COMFORTING GIFT. I HAVE THE ROOM, IN MY HOME AND IN MY HEART, IF SOMETHING IMPORTANT COMES ALONG."
> —JENNA SPESARD

Tiny-House Life Lessons

Downsizing is a journey, and along the way, my tiny house has taught me several important lessons about life, possessions and the idea of "home."

LESSON No. 1
The funny thing about minimalism is that it's not just about getting rid of stuff—it's also a mentality that can be used in all aspects of life. Clearing the clutter in my home, as well as my mind, has been an enlightening experience. Through downsizing I have found solutions to problems I never realized I had, and I've created room in my life for the things that matter.

LESSON No. 2
Living small isn't exactly easy. In fact, it can be quite challenging. When I encounter a new problem—like a broken water heater—I now put it in perspective and the stress melts away. It's in the most testing times of our lives that we learn the most.

LESSON No. 3
One of the most important lessons my tiny house has taught me is to appreciate empty space. We have the urge to fill the empty space in our lives with things we don't need. But empty space is precious. I cherish the empty space in my home, and I protect it as well.

🏠 GOING MOBILE

HAPPY HOMEOWNERS
Tish (left) and Erika Campbell relax with their dog, Ani, alongside their self-built tiny house.

Can we actually do it? That's a primary question that future tiny-housers often ask when deciding whether to build a small home themselves or hire it out. That was certainly the case for Erika and Tish Campbell, as neither of them had any construction experience before the start of their build.

But Erika and Tish were intrigued by the lifestyle after seeing photos of blogger Macy Miller's "Minimotives" tiny house on wheels (see Macy's story on page 24). Passionate about travel and the outdoors, they decided to build their own tiny house and to align their daily lives with their core values.

"We don't subscribe to the ideal that one must dedicate 50-plus years of hard work in order to enjoy retirement," says Erika. "We do our best to make choices that support our daily happiness now."

Another attractive benefit to the duo was the idea of being able to own a home without having the stress of paying a mortgage for years (or even decades). Pricing out the total cost of

108 THE GIANT BOOK OF TINY HOMES

275 SQUARE FEET

DIY Tiny

No experience? No problem! Research and determination gave this Portland, Oregon, couple the confidence to build a cost-conscious tiny house

CLOSE BY
Squeezed into its legal urban lot, the Campbells' tiny house is steps away from its neighbor.

GOING MOBILE

UNLIKE A TRADITIONAL HOME, A HOUSE ON WHEELS CAN BE STOLEN. PREVENT THIS BY USING WHEEL LOCKS OR HOUSE BLOCKS.

The barn-style door closes for bathroom privacy. Open, it hides the shelves at the end of the kitchen counter.

WAKE UP HAPPY
Skylights keep the loft warm, cozy and flooded with daylight.

A STEP UP
The tansu-like staircase doubles as a graduated series of storage cabinets.

LABOR OF LOVE
The Campbells worked through summer's heat, winter's cold and plenty of Northwest rain.

small construction—and using only high-quality, environmentally friendly building materials wherever possible—the couple came up with a target budget of just $55,000.

Once the commitment to go tiny was made, they tackled the educational process with fervor, attending two of tinyhousebuild.com's workshops (one in Orlando, Florida, and another in Portland), reading everything they could get their hands on, and affirming each step of the way that, despite their total lack of construction experience, they would indeed succeed.

🏠 GOING MOBILE

> STAY ORGANIZED: EACH DAY, BEFORE YOU BEGIN TO BUILD, TAKE TIME TO SET GOALS AND CLEARLY LAY OUT TASKS FOR THE WORK AHEAD.

SMOOTHING IT OUT
Walls made of ½-inch-thick sanded plywood are easy to install and paint.

112 THE GIANT BOOK OF TINY HOMES

• • •

"WE DO OUR BEST TO MAKE CHOICES THAT SUPPORT OUR DAILY HAPPINESS NOW."
—ERIKA CAMPBELL

• • •

From trailer delivery to move-in took 18 months. They had some help along the way from family and friends, but the only two tasks they hired out were the electric and gas line installation.

The Campbells found a legal spot to park their tiny home, taking advantage of recent zoning-law changes to squeeze it into a narrow side yard of a suburban lot in North Portland. In response to Portland's housing crisis, the city now allows one movable tiny house per residential lot. The arrangement has been a win-win: Tish and Erika have a place to call home, and the property owner enjoys the supplemental rental income.

The couple (and their dog) have been living in their self-built home for just over a year and absolutely love it. Erika shares, "It feels pretty surreal. As the build was in its final stages, I had to keep reminding myself that it wasn't just a project—it was our home and we'd be living in it. Our first night was full of smiles and many deep breaths of relief." ■

Frequent travelers, the Campbells devoted part of their cabinet space to stashing luggage.

An under-sofa pullout drawer turns an out-of-the-way space into storage.

Want to Build Your Own Tiny House?

Get the confidence you need at the Digital Tiny House Workshop. Learn about codes and zoning, insurance, financing, design, construction techniques—even toilets and more—in this web-based workshop featuring 54 bite-size lectures totaling more than 13 hours of instruction. You can stream the classes from the comfort of your home when it's convenient for you. The team at Tiny House Build has put together a curriculum that's helped nearly 1,000 students rock their builds and live lives they've only dreamed about. Check out details at their website: tinyhousebuild.com.

GOING MOBILE

320 SQUARE FEET

Charlestonian Dreaming

A South Carolina couple builds a family-friendly tiny house with a look inspired by history

DIY TINY HOUSE PLANS RANGE FROM FREE (ONLINE) TO $750. CHECK STATE AND LOCAL CODES AND ZONING LAWS BEFORE YOU COMMIT TO BUILDING.

HAPPY HOME
Brimming flower boxes and beveled cedar siding—painted in upbeat colors—create a pleasant exterior.

It was a labor of love. And common sense. Moving to a 3-acre property in South Carolina, Chris Pate and his wife, Sheradan, wanted to establish a little secure cash flow for themselves and their two children. Although the acreage included a 2,000-square-foot house, the Pates decided to build a tiny house that they would live in so they could rent out the larger residence.

"I've always been fascinated with tiny houses and minimalism," says Chris. "I like the idea of financial freedom through downsizing." Living small has always had an appeal. "When I was a kid, I bought an old RV when everyone else bought cars. I loved the experience of living in a small space."

•••

"YOU CAN LEARN JUST ABOUT ANYTHING ONLINE, BUT THAT DOESN'T MEAN IT WON'T TAKE YOU 20 TRIPS TO THE HOME-IMPROVEMENT STORE TO DO IT."
—CHRIS PATE

•••

115

GOING MOBILE

STEP-UPS
A pullout drawer and hinged stair treads ensure the loft staircase does double duty with a closet and storage bins.

To keep construction expenses under control, the Pates decided to build their tiny house themselves. The only catch: They didn't have any building experience. Undaunted, Chris began to study tiny-house construction online. He taught himself to use a simple CAD program and began designing their tiny dream house in his spare time. When his drawings were finished, he sent them to a draftsman to ensure their accuracy.

With final plans in hand, the Pates bought a trailer and began to put together their tiny residence. The final design—8½ feet wide, 13 feet tall, and 24 feet long, with a simple shed roof and open floor plan—was especially family-friendly. A loft at each end created separate spaces for kids and adults, and Chris added a long "bridge" to connect the two spaces.

They gave themselves a seven-week window to complete the project. While they used the internet to learn building techniques, they eventually brought in an electrician and plumber to make sure systems were installed correctly.

"You can learn just about anything online," notes Chris, "but that doesn't mean it won't take you two weeks and 20 trips to the home-improvement store to do it."

Rainbow Row

The Pates adopted their exterior colors from Charleston's famous Rainbow Row, an iconic series of row houses located near the city's waterfront. The old houses, some dating back to the early 1700s, are each painted bright pastel colors and exemplify Charleston's architectural heritage.

THE GIANT BOOK OF TINY HOMES

CHOPPING BLOCK
The built-in-place kitchen counter is framed with 2x4s and topped with a made-to-order, walnut butcher-block countertop.

🏠 Going Mobile

A wooden bridge connects the kids' sleeping loft to the parents'. A hinged hatch, operated with a pull cord, opens for loft access.

LOFTS WITH LOW CEILINGS ADD LIVING AREA AND ARE LEGAL—BUT THEY TYPICALLY WON'T COUNT AS OFFICIAL "HABITABLE SPACE."

THE GIANT BOOK OF TINY HOMES

Natural wood accents and paneling add warmth to any home interior style.

Additional reinforcements arrived in the form of Chris' brother, Brandon, a professional builder from California, who helped out with finishing the interiors.

One of the most difficult decisions was what to do with the beautiful cedar-lap exterior siding. A natural finish was a strong possibility, but the Pates wanted something more unique. Sheradan chose a cheery bluish-green taken from the colorful houses of downtown Charleston. Black shutters and wrought-iron fixtures completed the historically inspired look.

With everyone pitching in, the Pates' goal of completing the project in seven weeks—and within a budget of about $50,000—was a reality.

"The hardest part was just managing everything," says Chris. "Making sure everything was done in the right order while keeping it all on budget. We jammed to get it done, and we love the result!" ∎

ROOM TO GROW
Open shelving in the bathroom makes this space feel light and airy.

119

CHAPTER 4

Backwoods Beauties

Filled with character and craftsmanship, these small cabins are a nature-lover's dream come true

This cabin sits pretty high above Lake Pend Oreille in the Idaho panhandle.

🏠 BACKWOODS BEAUTIES

When Pete Nelson was a young boy, his father built him a treehouse fort. As Nelson grew up, the thrill of that up-in-the-air playhouse never waned. In fact, it only got stronger, becoming a lifelong passion that would eventually turn into a business—Nelson Treehouse and Supply in Washington state. It's a family-run business that includes his wife, Judy, twin sons Henry and Charlie, and daughter Emily. Over the years, Nelson Treehouse has built hundreds of amazing treehouses all over the world. Many are fully habitable with kitchens, bathrooms, heating and air-conditioning.

We caught up with Nelson not long after he'd finished a special project—a treehouse for his son Charlie. The lofty abode sits on 23 acres that the Nelsons plan to turn into the Treehouse Resort and Spa, a nature retreat for wellness and relaxation. (The treehouse shown here is Charlie's.)

How Did You Get Started in the Business?

I went to school and got an economics degree, of all things, but I'm not a very academic kind of guy. In my economics classes, I was seeing people who were going to clearly just eat my lunch. So after I got my degree and met my wonderful wife, Judy, I became a builder for many years, building conventional houses. I loved working with my hands and I had an aptitude for seeing how stuff goes together. But I always had an interest in building grown-up treehouses, as I call them. I built my first grown-up treehouse in 1987. It was in my

"A LOT OF PEOPLE ARE SEEING THE BEAUTY AND THE JOY THAT TREEHOUSES BRING. IT'S A LEGITIMATE FORM OF ARCHITECTURE."
—PETE NELSON

A Nelson treehouse usually includes a winding staircase that adds a sense of whimsy.

TEAMWORK
Pete Nelson, right, confers with his son Charlie.

122 THE GIANT BOOK OF TINY HOMES

179 SQUARE FEET

Branching Out

A treehouse-building entrepreneur turns a boyhood dream into an amazing grown-up fantasy

🏠 BACKWOODS BEAUTIES

backyard and I enjoyed it immensely, but it was just more of a meditation room with a fireplace in it. After that, it was always my intention to create these wonderful places adults will enjoy.

Why Treehouses?
They're special in so many ways. They're places to relax and unplug and to be in nature with your own thoughts, if not with someone that you love and can be intimate with. They're the most enjoyable spaces. The idealized adult grown-up treehouse for me was always something rather simple—a bed to take a nap, a coffee maker and a desk to write love notes and poetry. And a deck. Of course, you've got to have a deck and windows galore because you've got to be looking out at the beautiful trees that you're in.

How Do You Pick the Right Spot for a Treehouse?
A treehouse can last as long as the tree itself and we tend to pick long-living trees like Douglas

ROOM ON TOP
Interiors include space for quiet relaxation. Many have running water and fully equipped kitchens (left).

Massive steel girders are the foundation of the support system that secures a treehouse to its airy perch.

firs, cedars and oak trees. There are oak trees in England that are 800 years old, and if you take care of your tree and your treehouse, they'll last a really long time.

How Do You Make Sure the House Is Secure Up High?

Trees grow mainly at their tips, so they're getting taller and they're getting wider. Generally, they're just getting fatter. Every year they put that ring on. They grow, but they also move and they move in the wind, so when you're going to connect to living trees you've got to keep those principles in mind.

For a typical treehouse, which involves multiple trees, you're going to connect one tree to the next with a beam. That beam is going to sit upon these big bolts that we call treehouse attachment bolts. They're essentially a perch, like an artificial limb. We put attachment bolts into the side of the trees and then we perch big beams on those bolts, spanning from one tree to the next.

The connection can be dynamic in that it lets the tree move and grow but the treehouse structure stays rigid and in place. Our structures get reviewed from an engineering perspective and plans have to have an engineer's stamp on them to make sure the treehouse we're planning will be safe and structurally sound.

How Do You Protect the Environment When Building the Houses?

There are ways of doing it responsibly. When installing the hardware, we make sure it's a tight fit so that there are no gaps. It's remarkable how

125

🏠 BACKWOODS BEAUTIES

the tree responds to that initial hole that you drill and then fill with the hardware. Although different trees have different strategies, physiologically they send sap to the wound right away. As they continue to grow, they add what arborists call reaction wood around that wound to make sure that no pathogens are getting in. As these trees get greater in girth, that connection with the hardware gets reinforced and stronger. The trees self-engineer. It's amazing. From an engineering standpoint, they're absolutely extraordinary.

What Was It Like Building a Treehouse With Your Son Charlie?

Oh my God, the best. I have two sons. They're twins. Henry is Charlie's brother and he's out in the field being a lead guy scheduling the countertops and the HVAC and on and on. Charlie is more of the carpenter and he's remarkably talented. I'm so grateful for that time with both my boys. I feel like one of the luckiest dads in the world. ∎

For more information about the Nelsons' Treehouse Resort and Spa, go to nelsontreehouse.com/treehouseresortandspa.

• • •

"FROM AN ENGINEERING STANDPOINT, TREES ARE ABSOLUTELY EXTRAORDINARY."
—PETE NELSON

• • •

HANGING OUT
Decks are essential for relaxing high in the trees. Real windows and doors elevate treehouses' style cred (above).

Some Lofty Ideas

Want to live the high life? Nelson Treehouse has great ideas on how to do that. A portfolio of its work includes (clockwise from upper left): the fully furnished Chapelle, a rentable unit at Treehouse Utopia in Texas; a multilevel, 297-square-foot hideout, also in Texas, nestled in a sprawling oak; a fairy-tale turret that welcomes you to this 600-square-foot perch in Maine; and a 285-square-foot beauty that sits 18 feet up in a silver maple tree in Washington state

BACKWOODS BEAUTIES

Location, location, location: A pier extending into the property's pond makes a soothing getaway spot.

THE LOOK MAY BE RUSTIC, BUT UNFINISHED MATERIALS, SUCH AS CORRUGATED SHEET METAL AND OLD BARN SIDING, ARE MAINTENANCE-FREE.

336 SQUARE FEET

Sweet Salvage

A Texas builder creates a cabin made of sustainable, reclaimed materials

BACKWOODS BEAUTIES

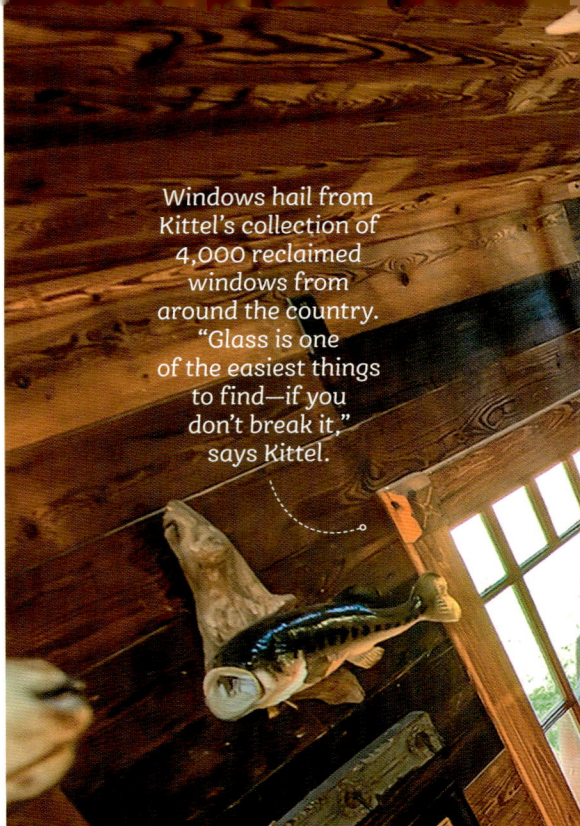

Windows hail from Kittel's collection of 4,000 reclaimed windows from around the country. "Glass is one of the easiest things to find—if you don't break it," says Kittel.

SCREENED OUT
The enclosed porch is ideal for mosquito-free lounging.

FUEL EFFICIENT
A single oil heater has warmed the Cowboy Cabin for less than $50 a month. The windows create a self-cooling system that keeps the house in a comfortable range throughout blistering Texas summers.

130   THE GIANT BOOK OF TINY HOMES

YOU CAN FIND VINTAGE HARDWARE, APPLIANCES AND BUILDING MATERIALS BY SEARCHING FOR "ARCHITECTURAL SALVAGE" ONLINE.

Darby Kittel takes a big step for the planet when he constructs tiny homes out of reclaimed materials. His "Cowboy Cabin," 95 percent built from salvaged material, is a great example.

"Why not?" Kittel says when asked why he gives old materials a second life. "I don't have to cut any trees. I'm using trees that were 500 years old when they were cut down, 150 years ago. I work with the hardest, strongest wood there is, which you can't even buy anymore."

Kittel was formerly president and founder of Tiny Texas Houses, a company that constructed tiny homes built almost exclusively with reclaimed materials. The company retrieved its building materials by deconstructing old homes and barns throughout Texas and as far away as Buffalo, New York.

BACKWOODS BEAUTIES

Nails, shot from souped-up nail guns, are one of the few new materials in the Cowboy Cabin.

> •••
> "I'M USING TREES THAT WERE 500 YEARS OLD WHEN THEY WERE CUT DOWN 150 YEARS AGO—THE HARDEST, STRONGEST WOOD THERE IS."
> —DARBY KITTEL
> •••

The Cowboy Cabin measures 12 feet by 28 feet and encompasses 336 square feet of living space. The main-floor kitchen comprises a prep island and living room. Two sleeping lofts rest on a second floor, which is accessible by two ladders that are integrated into the living room and kitchen shelving.

Much of the home is constructed with longleaf pine, a species native to the Southeast. The resin-soaked wood is rock-hard and naturally rot- and fire-resistant. It was so popular in the 1890s that by the 1920s, once-limitless longleaf pine forests were virtually gone.

Kittel salvaged the durable wood and coated it with nontoxic substances such as hemp oil, walnut oil and milk paint, a nontoxic paint made from milk casein and lime. "These bring out the color of the wood but don't outgas," Kittel says, referring to the volatile organic compounds that commercial paints and stains typically release.

Kittel was so enamored of reclaimed materials that he has created his own town—Salvage Texas—on 43 acres outside Luling. His vision is to offer a self-sustaining group of artists and elders living in 30 tiny homes constructed of second-life materials. Salvage Texas already hosts six homes. "We're making it into a paradise," says Kittel. "We're just looking for the right people." ■

The cabin is constructed of longleaf pine, salvaged from teardowns throughout the country, including Texas, Missouri and New York.

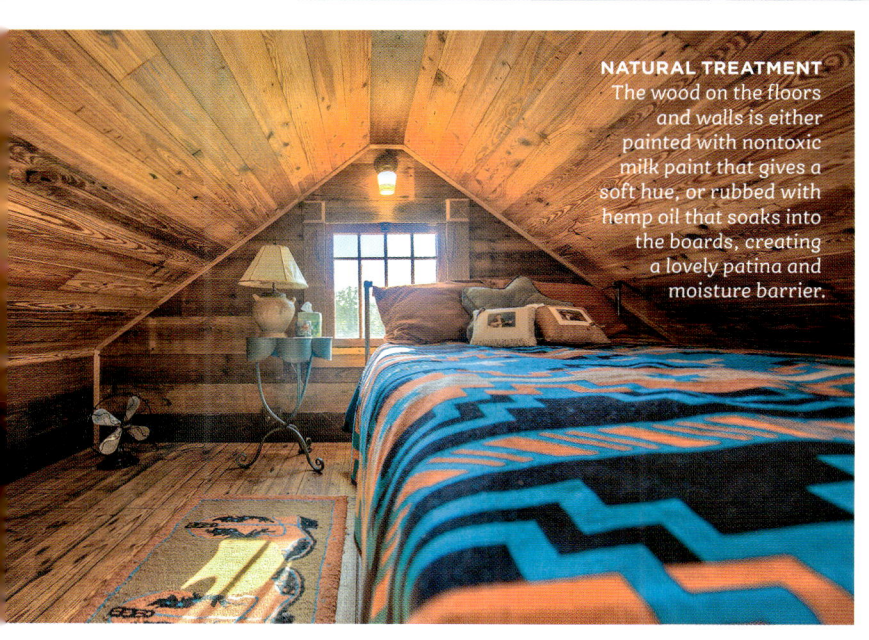

NATURAL TREATMENT
The wood on the floors and walls is either painted with nontoxic milk paint that gives a soft hue, or rubbed with hemp oil that soaks into the boards, creating a lovely patina and moisture barrier.

PATINA APPEAL
Primitive antiques, like this distressed-pine cupboard, are completely at home in these cozy surroundings.

⌂ BACKWOODS BEAUTIES

700 SQUARE FEET

Rock Star

Working within limits can yield surprisingly good results

NORTHERN IDAHO'S 45-MILE-LONG LAKE PEND OREILLE IS THE 38TH-LARGEST LAKE IN THE UNITED STATES.

ON POINT
A required 40-foot setback from the high-water mark made it clear that a tiny house was the only option for building on Lake Pend Oreille's Picard Point.

The rocky point jutting out into Idaho's magnificent Lake Pend Oreille offered seclusion, gorgeous views and wildlife highlighted by a nearby ospreys' nest. But was there enough room to build a house? Surveyors were called in to stake out the required setback distance from the high-water line. The result? There was space for a tiny house, but it wouldn't be a conventional rectangle.

"The 40-foot setbacks are what created the unusual 10-sided shape of the house," explains homeowner Chuck Hulbert. "It was a bonus that the footprint also gave us a wonderful 300-degree view."

Designer Eric Owens' final plans included cantilevered floors to gain more space and avoid having to dig too many foundation supports into the rocky cliff. "That gave us roughly 700 square feet to work with. But it was the limitation of setbacks that gave us the naturalistic shape of the house." That shape inspired Owens to design a roof that looks like an inverted leaf. Inside, the stem and veins of the "leaf"—replicated in laminated beams—give the tiny house a wonderfully organic feel.

And that stunning prow that juts out of the fireplace area? "That's the spine that forms the ridge of the roof," Owens explains.

BACKWOODS BEAUTIES

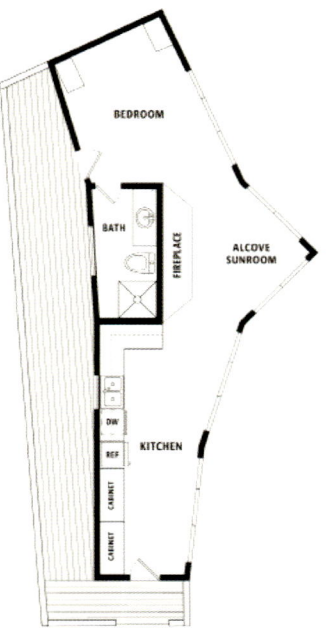

SMALL SCALE
Compact appliances make the kitchen serviceable without taking up too much precious space. The owners opted to forgo a dishwasher.

That type of timber framing requires precision, and Chuck is quick to praise the work of the builder, Jesse Watson of Golden Rule Construction: "He is an artist. The beams and rafters were tailored and honed until they fit just right with no gaps. He did an impressive job." Plenty of sliding doors and floor-to-ceiling windows add daylight and capture views of 20 miles of lake each way.

The challenging site required a year and a half of construction and plenty of problem-solving. The solid-rock point offered a firm foundation but meant using jackhammers to carve out a roughly 300-square-foot crawlspace for the electric forced-air furnace and service connections. Running electric, water and sewage lines required digging a 42-inch-deep trench out to the point. It leads from a stone-clad shed that holds a propane tank and generator to supply power to the house in the event of one of northern Idaho's fierce winter storms, and also for the pumps that keep the

ALFRESCO DINING
A stone patio made with rocks gathered from around the building site is the perfect spot for enjoying the views.

WARMING UP
A forced-air furnace located in a crawlspace beneath the house helps keep interiors toasty.

🏠 BACKWOODS BEAUTIES

"WE WANTED THE HOUSE TO BE AN OASIS WITHOUT IMPACTING ITS NEIGHBORS' VIEWS AT ALL."
—DESIGNER ERIC OWENS

The colorful living roof is made up of flowers planted in 600 individual trays.

STONE-FACED
A fireplace made of locally quarried stone acts as a divider between the living area and the bathroom.

Making a Living Roof

A rooftop garden begins by covering the entire roof deck with an impermeable material such as PVC, polyethylene or EPDM sheeting. Here, edging attached to the roof's perimeter holds 4¼-inch-deep plastic trays of lightweight soil.

Each tray is loaded with live plants and individually set in place. Succulents are among the preferred plants for living roofs because they are good at retaining water in intense sunlight. Grasses, wildflowers and other local wild plants can be good choices as well. In areas with long dry spells, some roofs need an irrigation system. Green-roof suppliers tout the long life of their roofs—up to 40 years—against the 20 years of a typical shingled roof. Green roofs also absorb sound, release oxygen and offer habitats for butterflies and songbirds.

water system going. "That trench later became the path leading to the entryway of the house," Owens says.

The green roof created challenges too. It hosts a variety of drought-tolerant grasses and sedums, succulent plants good at withstanding the hot and dry conditions of a rooftop.

"Geese like the plants on the roof," Chuck says with a laugh. "Doing what geese do, they left behind a lot of weed seeds. Now the weeds are established, and I have to go up once a month in the summer to pull what I can out." A built-in sprinkler system waters the roof during the height of summer.

The finished home is a retreat for owners Chuck and Pam. "We call it The Point," says Chuck. "It's a great place to have friends over for drinks or cards. I enjoy it as a place to read." He's catching up on philosophy and history—"stuff I ignored when I was younger," he says. "The beauty and quiet sure encourage contemplation." ∎

🏠 BACKWOODS BEAUTIES

COVER UP
A corner of the house serves as a shelter for the entryway. Seeds for the grass roof were gathered on the property.

To get to this Eagle Point cabin, you walk a narrow, unpaved path that meanders around knobs of granite and clumps of snowberry and then tucks underneath long, droopy limbs of Douglas fir. There's no parking nearby. Instead, there's a calming stroll that's designed to help shed the hustle and bustle of everyday life, and to ease into a simpler mode.

"The client is a very thoughtful, conscious person in everything she does," notes Geoff Prentiss, designer of the cabin and principal at Prentiss Balance Wickline Architects in Seattle. "She's very much into creating peaceful surroundings."

In keeping with his client's predisposition toward modesty and restraint, Prentiss designed a rectangular, 715-square-foot, two-room house with a shed roof. Although the design may be on the quiet side, the site isn't. The house nestles on Washington's San Juan Island, with spectacular views looking southwest across the glimmering Haro Strait to Canada's Vancouver Island.

"We could have put it closer to the water," says Prentiss, "but to take advantage of the uniqueness of the site, we kept it back. By doing so, the house also has total privacy from neighbors."

A large expanse of divided-light windows frame the views from the inside, while outside,

> SHED-STYLE ROOFS BLEND SIMPLICITY AND PRACTICALITY BY CREATING MODERN LINES AND HELPING REDUCE COSTS OF CONSTRUCTION.

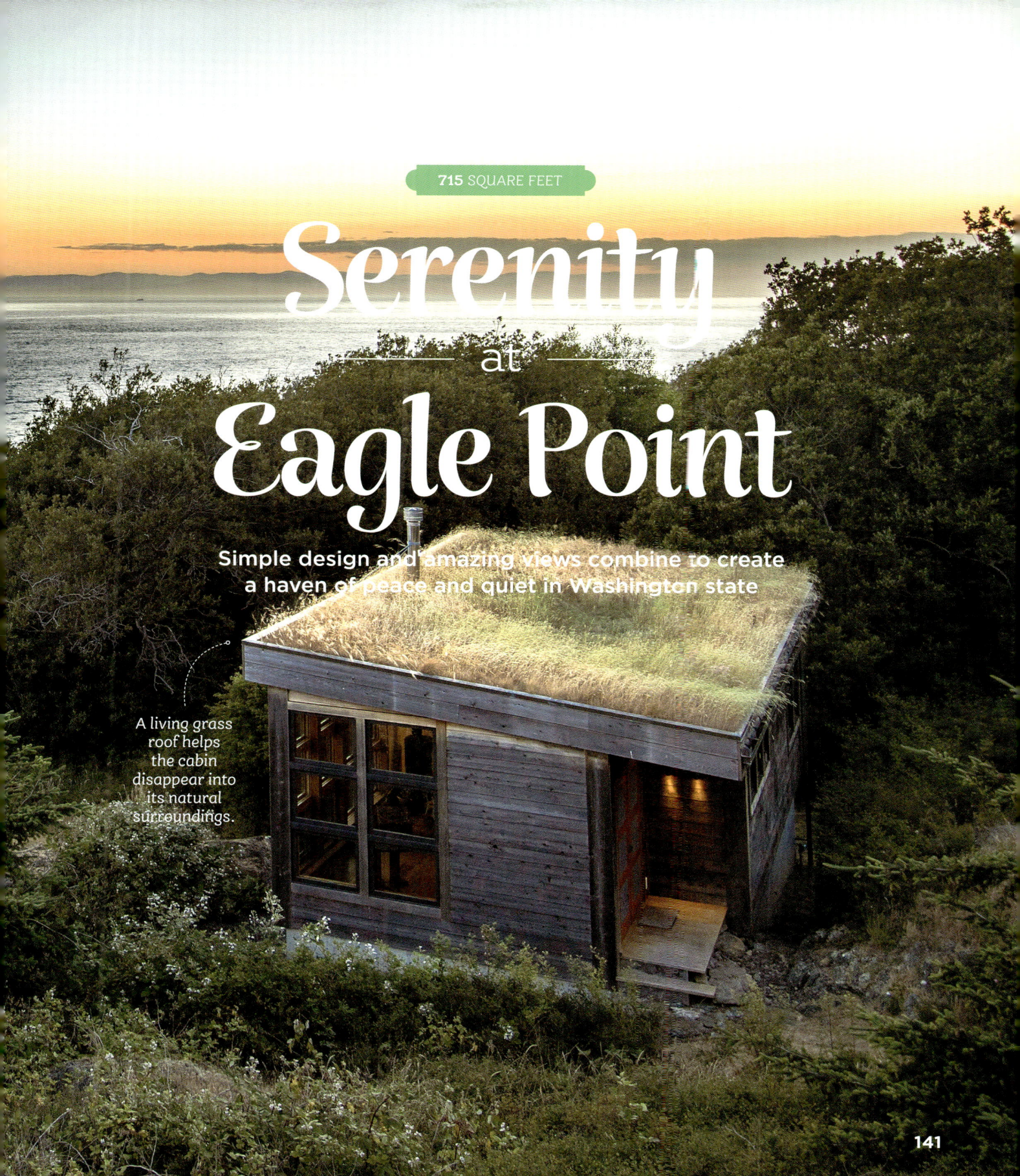

715 SQUARE FEET

Serenity at Eagle Point

Simple design and amazing views combine to create a haven of peace and quiet in Washington state

A living grass roof helps the cabin disappear into its natural surroundings.

141

🏠 BACKWOODS BEAUTIES

An open wooden planting shelf separates the living area from the entry.

IN A SMALL HOUSE LIKE THIS, LITTLE LUXURIES—SUCH AS HIGHLY INSULATED, 8-INCH-THICK WALLS—ARE EASIER TO INCLUDE IN THE BUDGET.

SIMPLICITY REIGNS
The streamlined kitchen avoids upper cabinets. The small undercounter refrigerator runs on propane.

Plenty of books are a soothing substitute for electronic devices and connections.

COZY SPACE
Reclaimed wood flooring and a paneled ceiling add warmth and sustainability.

WALK ON IN
The curbless shower is accessible and easy to clean.

the house retains its purposeful austerity. There are no porches, decks or gazebos. "It's about engagement," says Prentiss. "When the homeowner steps outside, she becomes totally immersed in the surroundings. There are no transitional 'outdoor living' areas."

Throughout, carefully chosen quality materials, finishes and fixtures provide elegant tranquility. Reclaimed wood floors and ceiling, plus wood trim, doors and wood-faced cabinets, are set off by clean, white walls. There is a bookshelf, simple furnishings and a narrow room divider at the entry. A lack of upper kitchen cabinets keeps the interiors serene.

Outside, unfinished cedar siding will age naturally and help reduce maintenance. A living roof, planted with seeds gathered from the property, tops off the natural setting.

Energy efficiency was a primary design goal. Walls are framed with 2x8s to achieve high R-values (for insulation efficiency), and orientation of the house toward the southwest means substantial solar gain. Although there's a small wood stove in the corner of the living area, it's rarely needed.

"The house has a great sense of place," says Prentiss, who was raised on San Juan Island. "It fits its environment beautifully." ∎

🏠 BACKWOODS BEAUTIES

860 SQUARE FEET

The Bootstrappers

A pair of Seattle-based architects combine beauty with practicality in their eastern Washington getaway cabin

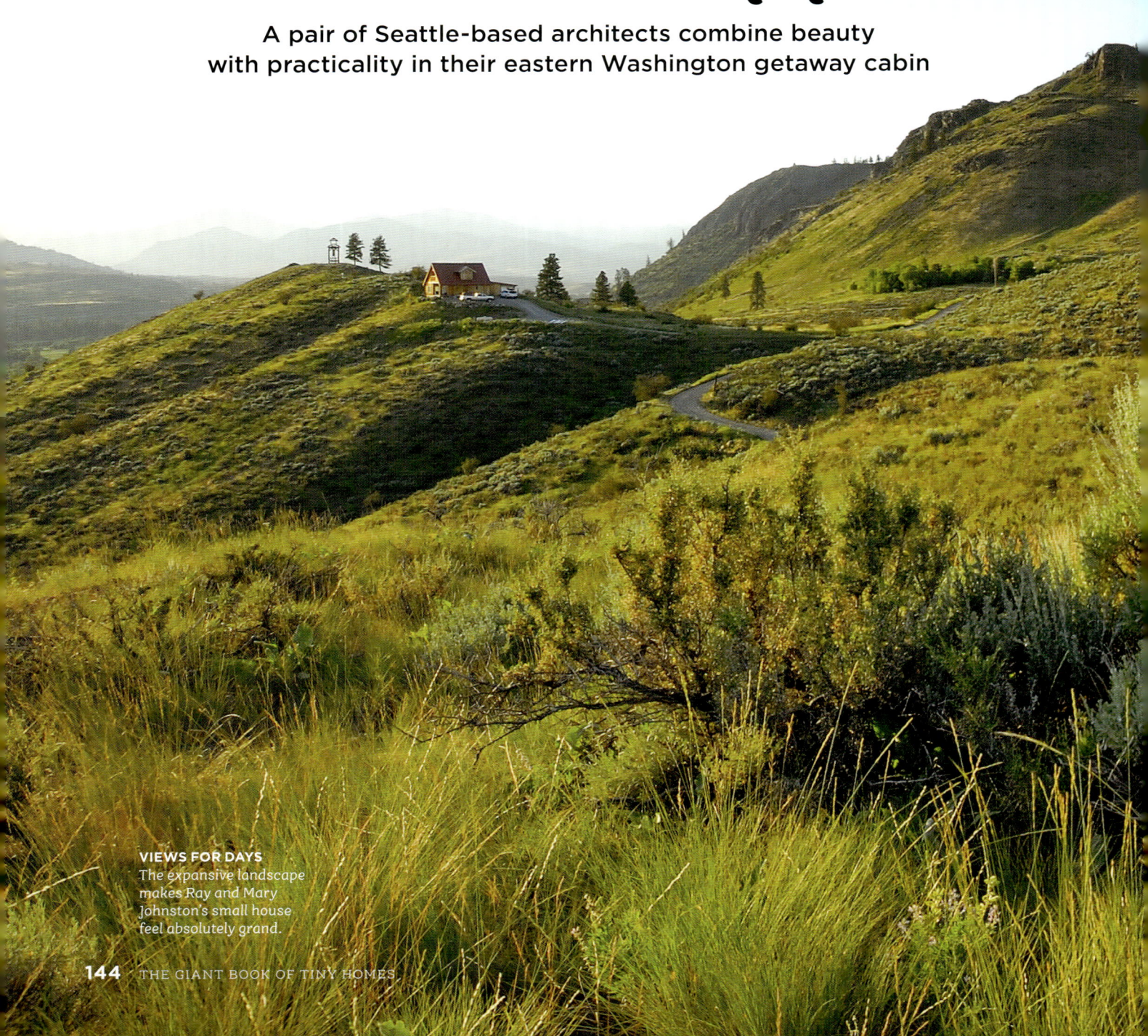

VIEWS FOR DAYS
The expansive landscape makes Ray and Mary Johnston's small house feel absolutely grand.

144 THE GIANT BOOK OF TINY HOMES

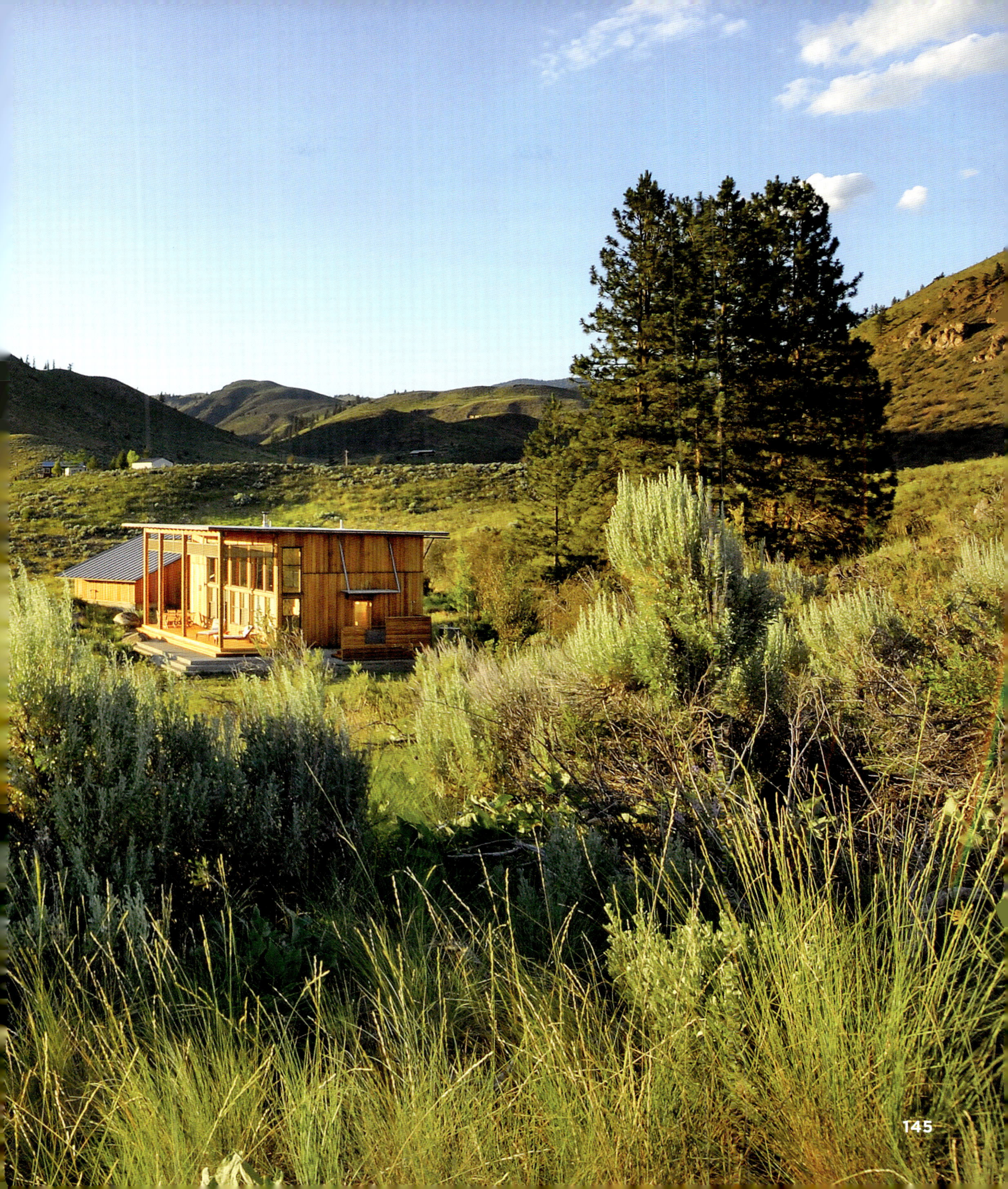

BACKWOODS BEAUTIES

STRETCHED OUT
The open-plan design gives the home a spacious feel.

COOKED UP
The kitchen was one place where the duo didn't want to compromise on size.

Mary and Ray Johnston, founding partners of their Seattle design firm, Johnston Architects, first became acquainted with the Methow Valley in Washington state years ago when they stayed on some land owned by a friend and client. They became enchanted with the area's sprawling mountains and clean, clear rivers, and decided that one day they'd build a cabin there.

Eventually they bought a piece of land with a spectacular view, but they didn't jump into building something right away. They couldn't —they were keeping a close eye on finances, and a new house just wasn't in the budget.

"We really bootstrapped everything back then," says Ray. "We bought a beat-up old Airstream and set it on the site so we could visit and think about things. And we thought for quite a while."

THE GIANT BOOK OF TINY HOMES

ROOM TO RELAX
Wide eaves protect a generous front porch that extends the living area and is perfect for alfresco dining.

147

🏠 BACKWOODS BEAUTIES

•••

"THE GOAL WAS TO HAVE A SMALL FOOTPRINT AND EXPLORE THE POSSIBILITIES OF A SIMPLE BOX."
—RAY JOHNSTON

•••

That contemplative interlude would be to their benefit, as they got to know the property "in all seasons and at all times of day," notes Ray. And that knowledge helped them make a confident choice for a building site, which ultimately became an area tucked up against a copse of pines with big views of the Cascade Mountains and the Methow River winding its way below.

When the couple did begin to draw and build, they remained mindful of economy. Construction proceeded step-by-step, with site prep, foundation work and framing moving ahead whenever they had a little extra cash.

The basic design evolved to just over 800 square feet, using the most cost-effective shape—a large rectangle with a nearly flat shed roof. Inside, a soaring ceiling rises over 16 feet and adds a sense of volume and expanse, and a wall of floor-to-ceiling windows opens up to the views beyond and add to the feeling of being in a much larger space.

Working within the modest footprint, the architect duo strategized how to maximize what space they had.

HAPPY HOMEOWNERS
The Johnstons didn't want to compromise on size.

"We envisioned having people here, friends and family, so we tried to strike a balance between keeping things small but at the same time making spaces where people can hang out," says Mary. "They didn't necessarily have to be rooms with doors, but more like alcoves where you can be alone or get a little work done."

THIS HOUSE IS ABOUT CONTRASTS: BETWEEN INTIMATE SPACES AND EXPANSIVE ONES, BETWEEN MATERIALS THAT ARE SLEEK AND ONES THAT ARE ROUGH.

ALL AROUND
Windows on the west side are 15 feet tall to maximize the view of the sky, valley, river and Cascade Mountains.

Case in point is the "master bedroom," an 8-foot-square space on the first level that's conveniently tucked away behind a sliding door. The couple also took advantage of the high ceilings to add a loft with two small upstairs bedrooms and a bathroom, so guests would feel comfortable visiting their home.

"Our first holiday season we had nine people here," says Mary, "and we made it all work. That was a memorable holiday!"

All during the process, value engineering was a constant mantra. "This became like a little laboratory for using inexpensive materials that you wouldn't necessarily see in other residences,"

BACKWOODS BEAUTIES

says Mary. "Things we could develop and show clients at a later time." They used inexpensive bamboo-faced plywood to cover interior walls, and stainless steel mesh to create a railing system for the loft. Rather than cover the roof trusses, they left them exposed, cantilevering them 12 feet beyond the exterior wall to create a large covered front porch—another way to include inexpensive space.

Outside, small vegetable gardens beckon during the growing season. "We really enjoy the gardens," says Mary. "When you have a small house, if you can extend your living area into a garden and spend time hanging out there, it makes everything live a lot larger."

With their getaway house now well-established, Ray and Mary fully enjoy splitting their time between the big city and the idyllic charms of the Methow Valley.

"We've designed a lot of houses over the years," says Ray, "but this is one we got to live in and I love it. I love having people over and when they're here, they're delighted. It changes their view on what small houses can be."

Adds Mary, "I enjoy the discipline we used out of necessity to create this house. It made us see our designs as flexible and sort of timeless. It doesn't bother me at all how small it is, we're just so used to it. It just seems perfect." ∎

SHADED SPACE
Billowy, sheer curtains help mitigate the western sun during the warmer months.

1. Garage
2. Kitchen
3. Dining
4. Living
5. Bedroom
6. Bathroom
7. Pantry

150 THE GIANT BOOK OF TINY HOMES

REST AND RELAX
Only 8 feet square, the first-floor bedroom can be closed off with a sliding door.

BACKWOODS BEAUTIES

996 SQUARE FEET

Remote Possibility

Building an off-the-grid island retreat poses significant challenges but yields lifelong rewards

LOOKING OUT
Steel pins were drilled into the granite to provide stability for the timber-frame foundation. Discreet glass railings offer a safe perimeter without interrupting the view.

153

BACKWOODS BEAUTIES

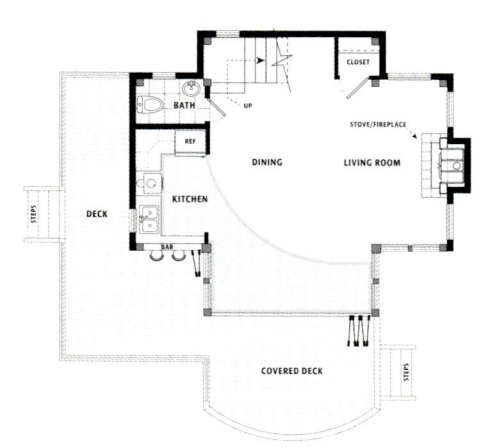

ORGANIC APPEAL
Douglas fir timber framing and boards form a beautiful golden interior for the cabin.

When your noisiest neighbors are humpback and killer whales spouting in the bay and the only "nearby" lights at night are the moon and stars, you know you're miles from civilization. Throughout the year, Brian Kingwell and Janine Vertone happily escape the bustle of Vancouver, British Columbia, embarking on a three-hour excursion to their tranquil Nelson Island cabin retreat, making the last hour of the trip by boat. "If we go by sailboat, it takes longer, of course," Brian says. "It really depends on how anxious we are to get there."

"There" is an 80-acre piece of paradise—mountainous hills blanketed in Douglas firs, craggy granite outcroppings, winding trails and a stream-fed 20-acre lake. Perched high on the rocky hillside, the getaway affords a breathtaking view of the rugged coastline and misty-blue ocean bay frequented by playful sea otters and pods of whales and dolphins.

When Brian and Janine purchased this wilderness wonderland, they knew the location was perfect for unwinding and refreshing from the workweek grind, but building a home on a granite hillside located so many miles from the mainland would call for ingenious problem-solving and precision planning.

NATURE EMBODIED
Granite quarried from nearby Hardy Island, and locally harvested Douglas fir, pair with expanses of glass to make the house a natural part of the remote setting.

ENGINEERING SOLUTION
Steps cantilever sans metal supports, keeping the look light and open. A wall of pebble tiles on the staircase adds natural color and texture.

BACKWOODS BEAUTIES

"We knew that even though we wanted a small cabin, it would still be a challenging place to build with no roads in, no power, no water," Brian says. "Brilliantly and beautifully conquering all those hurdles—that's really where Dave Petrina and his company, Kettle River Timberworks, shine."

Petrina and his team handled the project from concept to completion, designing and building the 996-square-foot cabin and devising smart solutions for solar-powered electricity and wood-burning heat. Brian came up with strategies for running water using a rainwater collection and filtration system, and equipping bathrooms with composting toilets.

A barge delivered the hefty load of construction and finish materials, including prefabricated timber framing, to the island, and a helicopter lifted the loads to the cabin site. "It was only 100 meters from where the barge moored up to the building site," Petrina explains, "but it was 100 *vertical* meters."

Even with all these hurdles, the cabin, although modest in size, offers an abundance of luxuries and "wow" design features, including a "floating" staircase, open-beam architecture, generous

• • •

"WITH REMOTE CONSTRUCTION, YOU CAN'T RUN TO THE HARDWARE STORE BECAUSE SOMETHING BREAKS OR YOU FORGOT SOMETHING."
—BRIAN KINGWELL

• • •

expanses of windows and skylights, a glass-topped deck roof and curved glass railings, and folding glass walls that blur the line between indoors and out.

"The beautiful woodwork is all locally harvested Douglas fir, so we're surrounded by a forest of the wood the home is built from," Brian says. "When we're here and the weather's good, the full-wall doors remain open, so even when you're inside, you feel like you're living in part of the forest. With all the glass, decks and open planning, we feel like the house is much larger.

"This really is a complete escape," Brian adds. "No city sounds, pristine forest—it's a complete getaway." ∎

NOTHING TO HIDE
In this remote location, privacy isn't a concern—so even the freestanding tub has plenty of views to the outside.

AU NATURALE
Skylights punctuate the master bedroom ceiling with sunlight and blue sky. Wall-size doors fold back to make the space part of the outdoors.

156   THE GIANT BOOK OF TINY HOMES

The perfect perch to watch for orcas and sea otters in the bay below.

Off-the-Grid Construction

"It's all about planning," says builder Dave Petrina. Here's how he pulled it off.
- Locally harvested Douglas fir timber framing was cut to size and drilled off-site, then delivered for assembly.
- Timbers, walls and all other building supplies traveled on two ferries to a barge, which transported the cargo to the island, where a helicopter off-loaded 26 tons of materials. "We had to time the barge's arrival to coincide with tides."
- Workers remained on-site to build the project, staying first on a sailboat and later in a wall tent. A crew of four working 12-hour days completed the house in about 75 days.

LIVING LARGE
Many tiny homes are built to incorporate elements of the great outdoors.

CHAPTER 5

The Tiny Home Life

Living with a smaller footprint means lower ownership costs, less maintenance— and more freedom to do what you love

🏠 THE TINY HOME LIFE

Best Plants
for Small Spaces

Enhance your indoor space with some greenery that will add color, filter the air and create a more natural feel

Bringing the outdoors in can help to liven up your tiny house, add fresh pops of color and detoxify the air inside your home. Succulents are a trendy choice right now, but other great options for interior spaces include air-purifying plants and those that grow well in low light.

> YOU OPTED FOR LESS SPACE SO YOU COULD LEAD A SIMPLER LIFE. LOOK FOR PLANTS THAT ARE EASY TO CARE FOR.

Indoor Plants That Clean the Air

Plants help improve indoor air quality thanks to their ability to turn carbon dioxide into oxygen. Some varieties are especially well-known for their purifying abilities and can improve the air quality in your home by getting rid of specific airborne toxins that can cause allergies and respiratory distress. "All green plants are air purifiers in the sense that they remove carbon dioxide," says florist and veterinarian Mary Alford, DVM. "But removing toxins is something additional that they can do."

Where to Put Indoor Plants

We already know that aloe plants go great in the kitchen, but where else should you place plants? Choose a spot that adds soothing greenery and dashes of color without overwhelming the space or detracting from your interior design.

•BATHROOMS Ferns like the moisture and humidity they absorb while you shower. And if you notice your ferns need more water, it will be easily accessible! You can position ferns in a pot on the vanity countertop or on a shelf near the shower.

•WINDOWS If possible, put bigger floral arrangements in front of large windows that are proportional to the length of the glass. Your plants will also receive the light they need to flourish.

•COFFEE AND KITCHEN TABLES Avoid placing large arrangements in areas used for socializing; they can be distracting or block your view. Smaller plants like bulbs or small succulents look great in the center of conversation areas. They will still add pops of color without getting in the way.

Plants That Thrive in Low Light

Proper sunshine is always a concern for indoor greenery—especially with limited space. However, there are plenty of plants that can thrive in low-light environments. Alford suggests going with ferns and orchids, especially Phalaenopsis, sometimes called the moth orchid, a flowering plant that does best in low-light situations. It also adds a vibrant pop of color to your space with its purple, white and orange flowers. The American Orchid Society recommends placing the orchid in an east window to get an ideal amount of sunlight. ∎

THE TINY HOME LIFE

Making the Most of a Tiny Garden

Find bounty for your table in 40 square feet

DIGGING DEEP IS EASIEST IN A RAISED BED—AND YOU WON'T COMPACT THE SOIL BY STEPPING ON IT. THE SOIL WARMS EARLIER IN THE SPRING, TOO.

RISE UP
Mound the center of your bed so the soil is 6 inches higher in the middle than at the edges. This can give your tiny garden a valuable 1½ square feet of extra growing surface.

A tiny garden can live big, but—like a tiny house—it takes planning and attention to detail. Do it right and you'll harvest a steady supply of fresh vegetables at a rate that won't overwhelm your storage (who has the space to store zucchini the size of zeppelins, anyway?). Here's how to get the most out of a 4-by-10 garden plot.

COLORFUL EDIBLES
Orient small beds so they face south, with taller plants toward the north so they won't cast shadows on shorter plants.

Double-Dig
Deeply aerated soil lets plants send their roots down instead of outward. The payoff: closer planting and greater drought tolerance. To double-dig, first excavate an 8- to 10-inch-deep trench with a shovel, then fork the bottom of the trench to loosen the soil another 6 to 8 inches. That will give the roots of your plants up to 18 inches of nicely aerated soil.

Pick the Best
Choose edibles that you love and are the most productive—and don't be shy about spending a little extra for top quality. Lean toward plants that flourish vertically when trained to a trellis, pole or tepee. Tomatoes and peas are obvious choices, but remember that vegetables like cucumbers and squash also do well as climbing plants. After all, that's what those little spiral tendrils are for!

Buying plant starts gives you a jump on the season. It's common to find tomato starts, but cucumbers, squash and even snow peas can be transplanted, too. The result can be as much as an extra month of productivity. Also consider growing microgreens. These immature versions of typical garden plants are planted from seed and then harvested early and throughout the growing season. Spinach, carrots, beets and radishes are a few that are tasty in their infancy.

Plant Strategically
Plant so that the tallest plants won't shade smaller plants. That typically puts tomatoes to the back of the garden and shorter plants, like spinach, to the front. In the dog days of summer, taller plants can provide useful shade—you could tuck a second crop of lettuce behind the summer squash, for example. Known as succession planting, this second sowing keeps limited space productive. In the late summer, kale and broccoli can be planted to yield crops well into the winter. ■

STRAIGHT AND NARROW
A string line helps keep planting trenches true to maximize space in the small garden.

SECOND CROP
Planting toward the middle of summer yields more food per square foot.

163

THE TINY HOME LIFE

Throwing a (Tiny) Dinner Party

These seven savvy ideas for small-scale entertaining will have your mouth watering

Fact: When converting to a tiny house, your lifestyle will change. You'll need to get rid of some things. You'll become more aware of the space you once occupied, for better or worse. Fortunately, there are just as many things that will not have to change. You can still bring your own sense of style into your home. You can still cook yourself meals whenever you want. And you can still have friends over and host dinner parties. Here are some simple tips and tricks to help you throw a fun gathering in your tiny space.

1 | Clear the Clutter
If you aren't planning on using a particular item for the party, put it away. You want to be able to take advantage of as much countertop area as possible.

2 | Take Advantage of Outdoor Space
If you are hosting your party in a warmer climate, consider having it outside. There are places where you can rent a table and chairs, if needed. Hang up some string lights and set up an outdoor speaker for a chill vibe. Just be courteous and let your neighbors know what you are planning.

3 | Keep the Menu Simple
Cooking big, extravagant meals is great, but it can be very labor-intensive for a large party. There's nothing wrong with a good cheese plate, a one-skillet dinner and ice cream sundaes for dessert.

4 | Make It a Potluck
Plan to cook the main dish and appetizers, but let some of your guests bring a side or dessert if they please.

5 | Serve Food That Requires Minimal Plates and Utensils
If there isn't a ton of room to sit and eat at a table, you need to ensure that you are serving food

WINE AND DINE
A little outdoor space goes a long way toward making guests comfy at your tiny house dinner party.

165

🏠 THE TINY HOME LIFE

KEEP IT SIMPLE
Pasta is easy and always a hit.

that can be eaten while standing up. That means nothing that needs to be cut or held with two hands. Side tables and countertops can help.

6 | Keep the Air Moving
Packing several people into a tiny space can result in limited air movement. Consider how you will cool the space.

7 | Designate an Area for the Stuff
Depending on the time of year, your guests may come with coats or other outerwear. Make sure you have a space to put them (like your loft) so that they're out of the way. You don't want to lose precious seating because everyone is throwing their jacket over a chair. ∎

Blog reprinted with permission from 84 Lumber's 84tinyliving.com.

•••
LET SOME OF YOUR GUESTS BRING A SIDE OR DESSERT.
•••

166   THE GIANT BOOK OF TINY HOMES

FINGER FOODS
Serve apps or main courses that can be easily eaten and enjoyed.

THE TINY HOME

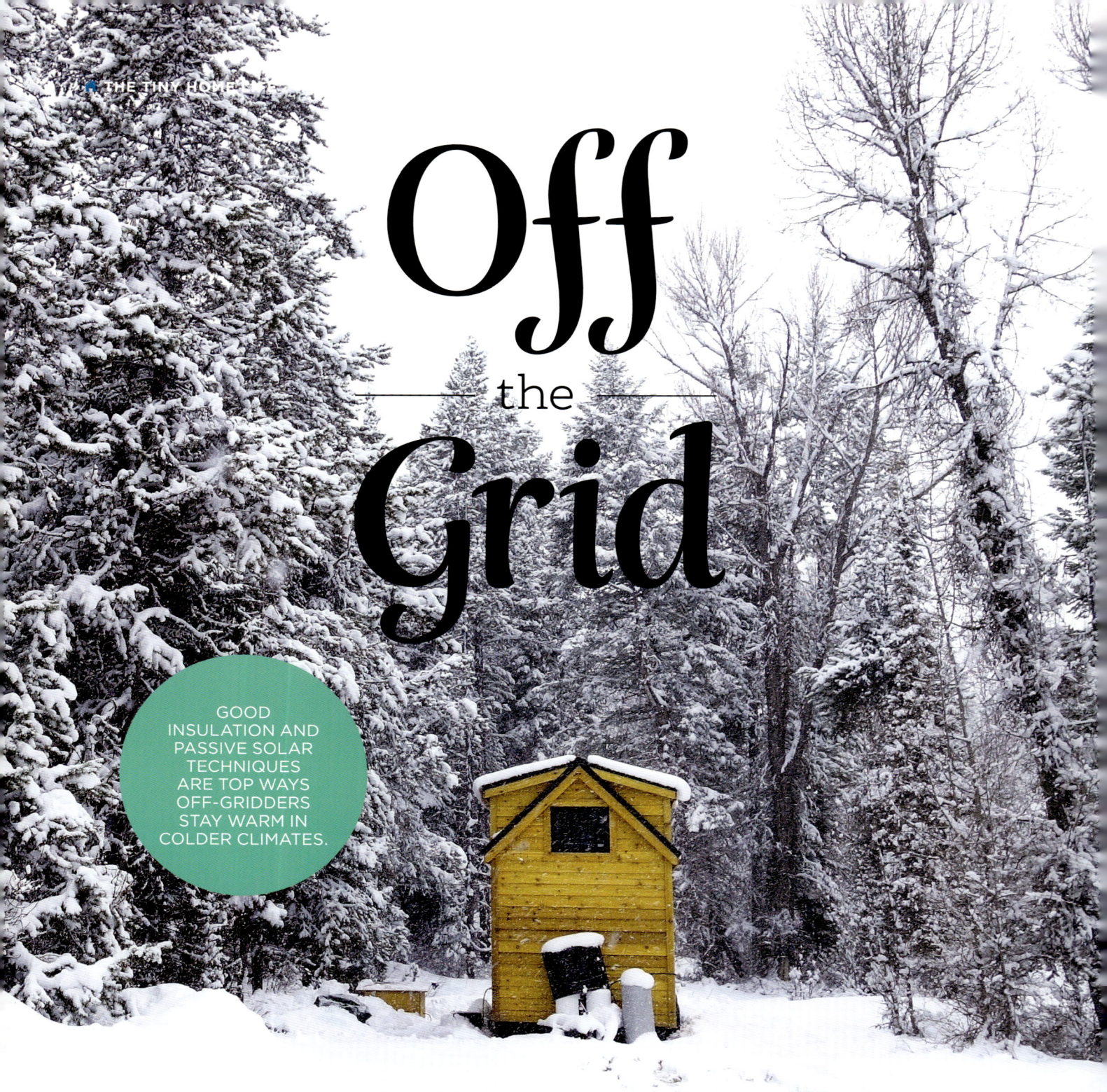

Off
— the —
Grid

GOOD INSULATION AND PASSIVE SOLAR TECHNIQUES ARE TOP WAYS OFF-GRIDDERS STAY WARM IN COLDER CLIMATES.

Living self-sufficiently offers the ultimate in independence. Here's what you need to know before you unplug, unhook and unwind

1
STORMY WEATHER
Stay Informed About Storms and Fires When You Are Way Off-Grid

An off-grid house offers independence, economy and, sometimes, the peace and quiet of isolation. But it might also mean you're out of range of cellphone towers and internet access—the information lifelines of on-grid life. In the wild, it's still vital to have ways of communicating.

Ham It Up
The old-school option is amateur (aka ham) radio. Even though it's been around for more than a century, nothing quite equals its universal reach. Pioneered in Australia (where they really know what it's like to be isolated), ham is more than just a hobby for those who love the warm glow of vacuum tubes. It's a lifeline for many, providing medical diagnosis, schooling, linkups with loved ones and, of course, emergency news. In fact, when a disaster strikes and all other lines of communication are down, ham operators often become the only means of relaying ever-changing conditions to first responders.

Amateur radio is not a plug-and-play option, however. You'll have to study for an operator's license and learn some basic radio electronics. You do not, however, have to learn Morse code as most ham operators once had to (by the way, the term "ham" arose from the "ham-fisted" efforts of newbie Morse code practitioners). You'll also have to buy a radio set. A handheld unit can start as low as $40.

You may also be able to get by with a CB radio. However, its range might be as little as 1 mile (some locales offer a range of up to 25 miles). The positive here is that no license is required, but that also leads to its downside: The airways are almost always crowded. You may have a hard time getting crucial information when you need it most.

Kiss the Sky
For a new-school option, consider a satellite phone. It'll set you back $250 to $1,750, with costs depending on durability and features like internet access. "The satellite phone itself is pricey," notes Greg Parham, owner of Rocky Mountain Tiny Houses in Durango, Colorado. "But you only pay as you use it." Typically that's $6 to $9 per minute, with no long-term contract required. All you have to do is register with a satellite provider.

To use the phone you need a clear view of the sky (the point being that you need to connect with a satellite). You tap in a number for your country, your satellite provider and finally the number you're calling. And just who might you need to call? For weather, use the National Weather Service number for your region. For forest fire updates, call the National Interagency Fire Center at 208-387-5050.

MAKE THE CALL
Many satellite phones weigh only a few ounces and are about the same size as a cellular phone.

169

THE TINY HOME LIFE

2

WHEN NATURE CALLS
Choosing an Off-Grid Toilet

Dealing with human waste is one of the more challenging decisions you'll face as an off-gridder.

The Compostable Choice

Thorough composting cooks out pathogens and viruses in human waste, making it safe for nourishing trees and bushes (but not for vegetable gardens). There's no flushing, so it saves thousands of gallons of water each year, too.

A composting toilet is easy to install, looks much like a conventional toilet and costs about $1,000. Use it like a regular toilet, except shut a trapdoor to send urine to a tank and open the trapdoor so solid waste falls into a chamber. A fan-powered vent pulls fresh air in and pushes odors out. Instead of flushing, add peat moss or sawdust to the waste, then crank the composting chamber to mix it all for aerobic (oxygen-fueled) decomposition.

Does it work? Kinda, but "it's not flush and forget. It needs outdoor composting," cautions Parham. "In warm areas like Texas or Arizona, the waste will fully compost in six months. In colder climates it'll take more like a year." Some units include built-in heaters that encourage decomposition. Parham prefers an 80-gallon drum-type composter.

Disposal of toilet compost is a bit controversial. Some bury it in the woods; others put it with the garbage. "Just make sure it doesn't go into the water table," warns Raheel Alam, with Tumbleweed Tiny House Company in Colorado Springs.

The Outhouse Revisited

"It's an option many people never think of," says Jeremy Weaver, co-founder of Wind River Tiny Homes in Chattanooga, Tennessee. And an outhouse doesn't have to be the smelly, cold box-over-a-pit of yore. "Put in a skylight and a heater and burn some incense." While a privy may not be the best solution in subzero winters, it's a viable option, especially if you're on a limited budget. Experienced outhousers recommend a pit at least 6 feet deep. Good venting and an inexpensive solar-powered fan can help keep odors at bay. Check local codes and zoning regulations before you dig—some areas have strict requirements for pit toilets, especially regarding proximity to waterways. Those regulations also can provide useful instruction for proper construction and venting.

Some Like It Hot

If you don't want the hassle of dealing with your composted waste, consider an incinerating toilet ($2,000–$6,000). Powered by propane, it looks more like a kiln with a seat than a conventional toilet. Using it is straightforward, with one exception: As waste is deposited, spray an odor-limiting foam on it. That way, you can accumulate deposits before firing the unit up. When the holding chamber is full, lift the seat and place a fireproof cap on the chamber, then ignite the incinerator. After a couple of hours the load is reduced to a few spoonfuls of sterile ash.

A Whole-Hog Septic System

Eco-friendly and virtually fuss-free, a septic system lets you use a regular low-flow flush toilet. Local codes may require you to install a septic system at a cost of $3,000 to $5,000, but Weaver notes that in some parts of the country there are no regulations. "There are plenty of self-engineered septic systems that work fine," he says.

PRIVY PITS Digging at least 6 feet deep should be good for about five years of use.

> ONLINE SOLAR CALCULATORS CAN HELP DETERMINE WHAT KIND OF SOLAR ARRAY YOU'LL NEED IN YOUR LOCALE.

3

HERE COMES THE SUN
What It Takes to Go Off-Grid With Solar Power

Cutting the umbilical cord to the power company is the defining step of going off-grid. If you're ready to take the plunge, you have three alternative sources for generating electricity: wind, water and sun.

The first two options have limitations. A wind turbine requires a stiff breeze, which is not available everywhere. Water—the micro hydro option—depends on nearby rushing water, again something not every site offers. And both require expensive kits.

That leaves sunlight. To one degree or another, it's everywhere. But is it the right choice for you?

Evaluating Your Site

Summer in Arizona will keep your solar panels humming all day long, topping up your batteries and even providing enough electricity to run an air conditioner. However, winter in Maine might leave you sunless for weeks on end, draining your reserve electricity when cold weather is at its most extreme. All sites require a system that takes best advantage of available sunlight and is set up to see you through the inevitable dark days.

To assess your locale, you can search online for a solar sunlight map, but it's easier to use one of the online calculators offered by solar-equipment suppliers like the altE Store and Wholesale Solar.

🏠 THE TINY HOME LIFE

Solar arrays don't need to go on your roof; ground installations are easy to maintain and adjust.

Adopting an Off-Grid Mentality

When you're on the grid, your supply of electricity seems limitless. However, when you're dependent on a solar setup, what you have in your batteries is all you have to work with. Squander that, and you'll spend an evening in the dark.

Your most basic step is limiting the appliances you use. For example, anything that heats electrically—a hair dryer, a water heater—consumes lots of energy. Small-scale energy-efficient appliances are the best choice. And the fewer, the better.

"You won't be able to do all the things you are used to when on the grid," explains Weaver. "You always have to think about energy consumption."

Off-gridders learn little tricks, he notes. "You can turn off the fridge at night when you won't be opening it and the air is cool. You can even put the fridge on a timer so you don't have to worry about it." With time, orchestrating the use of your solar-harvested electricity becomes second nature. Keep an eagle eye on the weather forecast so you can anticipate cloudy periods when you'll be living off your batteries.

Some owners spring for expensive DC (direct current) appliances because that's the type of current that comes directly off the PV (photovoltaic) panels. That avoids having to convert DC power to the AC (alternating current) power used by most household appliances, saving the cost of installing an inverter to change the current. However, that savings comes at a price—a DC fridge can cost $1,000, whereas its AC counterpart might be under $150.

Putting Your System Together

Every solar setup uses the same basic components. Panels mounted on the roof or in a ground-level array harvest sunlight. Cables from the panels feed into a charge controller that senses when the batteries need topping up or when they don't. The batteries send DC power to an inverter that changes the current to AC. Finally, a set of breakers controls the various circuits in your tiny house.

Suppliers' calculators are the quickest way to get an idea of what you'll need. Often, one of the system kits offered by a supplier will do the job. If not, you can enlist their design team for a custom solution. The cost of a complete system plus installation for a tiny house runs from $6,000 for a very basic system to about $14,000 for an elaborate setup.

However, even the grandest system won't see you all the way through the cold doldrums of winter. Battery capacity drops with lower temperatures; this needs to be factored in when estimating how much reserve you have. "To preserve battery life, a lead-acid deep-cycle battery bank should never be cycled to less than 50 percent of capacity," warns Brian Levy, owner of Minim House in Washington, D.C. Those limitations mean that batteries can keep you running for a few days, but eventually you'll need a backup generator.

As much as you may loathe the idea of incorporating a gas-guzzling generator into your otherwise pristine solar plan when you are really out there on your own, many consider it essential. And forget about those loud, clunky units common at home centers. "What you want is a good inverter generator," says Weaver. "It produces clean power with something called minimal resonance disturbance that won't fry your batteries." Veteran off-gridders come to love these beer-cooler-size machines, so quiet that at low load you can hold a conversation next to one. They are portable, weighing only 50 pounds even when fueled up.

4
SPLISH, SPLASH
Getting Water When You're Off-Grid

The average American uses 80 to 100 gallons of water a day, much of it flushed down the toilet. Off-grid home dwellers often use less than 20 gallons a day because they have nonflush toilets, are frugal with their heated water and don't have a dishwasher.

But even that reduced amount has to come from somewhere—and once used, it has to go somewhere. Setting up a pure, reliable source of water should be your first priority when choosing a site for your tiny home.

Choosing a Water Source

A spring or stream is a huge bonus, but it has drawbacks as a water source. First, you have to get the water to your house. Hefting buckets of water to meet your daily needs is no fun. Setting up a 250- or 500-gallon plastic tank and trucking in water is a workable solution, but leaves you reliant on outside help. Unless you're willing to haul water by hand and invest in a serious filtration system, you'll need a well.

In some areas the water table is high enough that you can use a DIY rig costing around $1,000 to drive a pipe into the ground to reach water. But be careful—high water tables are also prone to contamination. Most shallow wells are best reserved for watering the garden.

WATER WORKS A small well can provide ample water for your needs, but may still require heavy equipment to install.

🏠 THE TINY HOME LIFE

The best solution is a professionally drilled well. A pro outfit uses an auger to bore a 6-inch-diameter hole deep enough to reach water, sometimes hundreds of feet. Into the hole goes a casing of steel or PVC pipe, then stabilizing grout is pumped around the pipe. A submersible electric pump goes inside the casing. Finally, the well is capped so subterranean gases can escape and pressure is equalized when the pump is working.

Drilling a well usually requires heavy equipment, so it's a good job to leave to the pros. The job should cost $15 to $30 per foot in typical conditions, $30 to $50 per foot in tough conditions. All told, a well can cost around $5,000.

Putting on the Pressure

Once the water is out of the ground, it needs help getting to your sink or shower. One option is mounting a plastic tank in the rafters of your house. That means running the well pump to fill the overhead tank, then having gravity supply the oomph for taking showers and using the sink.

Another option is to have your well supply water to a holding tank so water is ready when you need it. At the holding tank, you'll need another pump with a flow rate suitable to supply your faucets and showerhead.

For a reliable, constant supply of water, install a pressure tank. As water is pumped into the tank from the well, an internal diaphragm compresses, giving up to 40 psi (pounds per square inch) of steady water pressure. Holding tanks come as small as 2 gallons, although a larger tank won't require constant refilling, putting less wear and tear on the pump.

RELIABLE SOURCE
Pressure tanks are ideal for holding well water and delivering it to your house with good pressure.

Marine-style propane heaters, made for boats, are compact and will heat up to 1,000 square feet of living space.

5
JUST THE RIGHT TEMPERATURE
Keeping Warm…and Maybe Even Cool

The beauty of a small house is that it doesn't take much to heat and cool it—and that's good news if you're going off-grid. Proper solar orientation and good insulating techniques to trap and retain the heat are primary considerations. And when it comes to supplying heat or cooling, experienced off-gridders recommend two lines of defense—one that uses solar-powered electricity and one that doesn't. (See page 176 for more heating ideas.)

Love Those Passive Features

Passive solar gain is a terrific ally. Eaves should offer shade in the summer but not be so deep

> IN VERY DRY REGIONS, A PORTABLE EVAPORATIVE (AKA SWAMP) COOLER HELPS DROP INDOOR TEMPS 20 DEGREES.

that they limit sunlight in the winter. "The orientation of your home is very important," notes Weaver. "The long axis should be east-west and the short axis north-south." Shady awnings and breeze-capturing operable windows help orchestrate comfort. A little electricity can help—solar-powered fans make you feel cool in summer, and a solar-powered blackout shade on a skylight can prevent 40 percent heat loss and give you 60 percent heat gain.

Consider the Mini-Split

An energy-efficient electric mini-split heater/air conditioner ($250 to $600) can be a cooling friend when the summer sun is out and you're harvesting plenty of energy with your solar panels. In the summer, you can run the A/C for three to four hours at the hottest time of the day without running down the batteries, and a well-insulated home will hold that coolness for quite awhile. And the mini-split is good for sunny-but-cold winter days, too, when you're craving toasty warmth as you're curled up on the couch. This can be your first line of defense in the shoulder seasons when only a bit of heat or cold is needed.

Wood Is Good

Chop your own wood, and you're warmed twice: That old adage sums up the pros and cons of using a wood stove to heat your tiny house. Your fuel is free if you have plenty of trees on your property, but there is a fair amount of work in using wood to heat your off-grid home. In addition to splitting firewood, you also have to stoke the fire, clean out the ashes and make sure the chimney is free of creosote buildup.

"It's tricky to find [a wood stove] small enough for a tiny house," says Parham. "Most produce too much heat."

But the payoff is a cheering fire that produces wonderfully dry heat. Wood is a dirtier fuel than we'd like it to be, but you can get around this if you can find a small stove with a catalytic converter.

One thing you can't get around is the need to keep a wood stove stoked. In the winter, that rules out being gone from your house for more than a day. Do so and you are more than likely to come home to frozen pipes. A mini-split can keep things warm, but only as long as there is available power. Or, you can switch on the propane.

It's a Gas

A thermostat-controlled propane stove is a fuss-free heating option, and you'll find a good selection of stoves sized just right for a little house. You do, however, have to keep the propane tank filled—and swallow perhaps $20 in heating expense per month through the winter. Unlike with wood heat, you can leave your home unattended in winter by simply turning down the thermostat, safe in the knowledge that your heater will kick in to keep the pipes from freezing. By installing a 10-gallon propane tank, you should have enough to last a month before refilling—even including gas for cooking and heating water.

Avoid ventless propane stoves. "They produce a lot of water vapor, which can lead to moisture damage," Parham explains. "Direct vents pull in outdoor air for combustion and vent moisture and gases outside." ■

🏠 THE TINY HOME LIFE

Staying Toasty
in Extreme Cold

Smart planning and simple building fundamentals will ensure your tiny house stays warm when temps dip into the low teens and single digits

When winter roars in and you're ready to hunker down, you want to know that your tiny house is a snug little fortress of warmth and comfort. Thankfully, that's relatively easy.

If you know that you'll be parking in a cold climate, build with the highest R-value insulation possible. Fill wall, floor and roof cavities with the maximum amount of insulation they can take, and be sure to seal around gaps with caulk to prevent air leaks. Consider building with structural insulated panels (SIPs) that provide structural rigidity, high R-values and reduce thermal bridging that occurs with traditional stud framing. Install triple-pane windows if you can afford them. If your bottom-line budget is a concern, think about reducing the number and size of windows to help reduce heat loss.

As with all trailers, it's a good idea to skirt your tiny house to reduce heat loss through the floor. Skirting can be achieved in a variety of ways for a range of budgets. Straw bales are a highly energy-efficient and budget-friendly skirting. Other options include permanent solutions such as marine plywood, foam boards and vinyl fabric. If you're parked in a location with a lot of snow, you could pile it around your trailer to create an igloo-like skirt. Keep in mind you'll have to maintain this type of skirting as the snow melts.

You should have a sufficient heat source in your tiny home, and it's a good idea to have a backup option. Electric wall heaters can be used as a primary or secondary heat source. For off-grid heat, compact wood stoves and propane heaters are popular. Be aware fuel costs can add up if you are in a climate that drops below freezing on a regular basis, and you'll need a sufficient stash to ensure you can get through long stretches of cold.

The biggest challenge tiny-housers face during winter is freezing water. You should prepare your pipes well before the weather turns cold. This can be done by installing heat tape around your water lines. You can also replace your hoses with

BE PREPARED
With advance planning you'll easily weather the winter.

Marine-type propane heaters designed for boats are especially good for off-grid tiny homes.

electrically heated ones for the winter season. For off-grid options, you can design the inside of your home to include a refillable freshwater tank. You can also create a wastewater disposal system that is below the frost line. Finally, you should insulate any water source and exterior exposed pipes with insulating foam jackets, available at any home-improvement center or hardware store.

If you're parked in a location with famously cold winters and/or at a high elevation, your propane pressure could drop too low to properly power your propane appliances. To remedy, purchase a heat blanket for your propane tanks or insulate them with wraparound foam.

Over time, you'll create cold-season systems that work for your situation. If it's your first winter spent in a tiny house, remember that a learning curve is part of the process. Be patient when things go wrong, learn from your mistakes and look to find creative solutions. ∎

🏠 THE TINY HOME LIFE

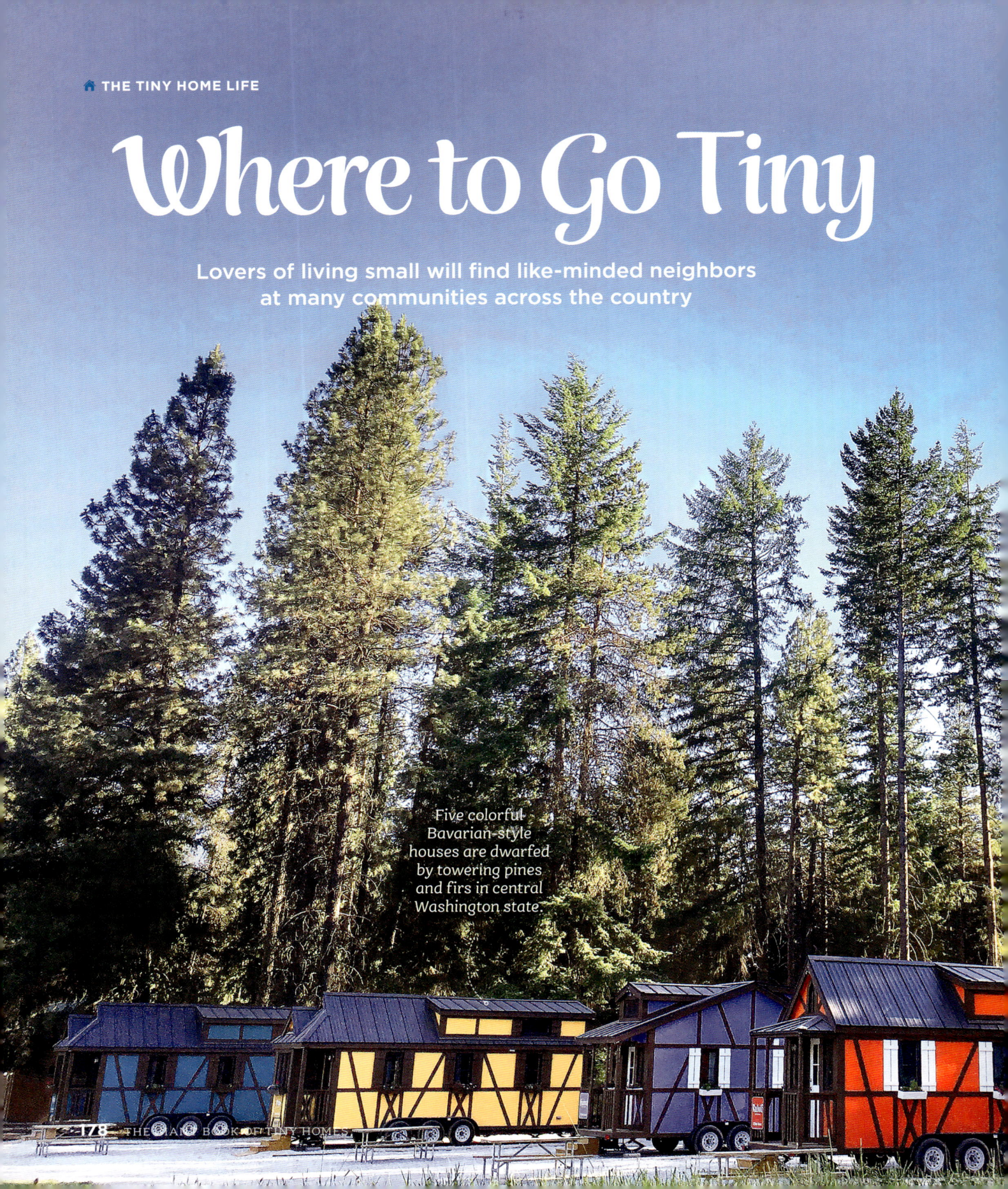

Where to Go Tiny

Lovers of living small will find like-minded neighbors at many communities across the country

Five colorful Bavarian-style houses are dwarfed by towering pines and firs in central Washington state.

As tiny house living becomes more widespread and normalized, villages designed especially for small-home aficionados are becoming increasingly popular and in-demand. Many of these villages have permanent residences that can be purchased or rented, plus spaces for those interested in moving their own tiny house onto temporary sites for days, weeks, months and longer. Here are some of our favorites.

TRY ON
Short-term rentals let you explore how it feels to live tiny.

Leavenworth Tiny House Village
Leavenworth, Washington

LOCATION Central Washington state, near osprey habitats, ski areas and wineries.
FEATURES The Cascade Mountains and Alpine Trout Lake provide hiking, fishing and kayaking in a Bavarian-themed resort that rents 180- to 300-square-foot tiny houses year-round.
WHO GOES THERE Outdoorsy types interested in all things Bavarian—architecture, festivals, restaurants, galleries and specialty shops.
COST $129–$149/night.
CONTACT 20752 Chiwawa Loop Rd., Leavenworth, WA 98826 **Phone** 888-229-5445
Web leavenworthtinyhouse.com/home

🏠 THE TINY HOME LIFE

This 399-square-foot model has a bedroom, a sleeping loft and built-in bunk beds —it can sleep eight.

Creek Walk Tiny Home Community Travelers Rest, South Carolina

LOCATION Minutes from Greenville, once a Cherokee hunting ground and now one of the fastest growing cities in the U.S.

FEATURES Cottage and tiny home village on the 22-mile Swamp Rabbit Trail, a multiuse greenway system for bikers and walkers. The trail also hides 125 "geocaches"—treasures you can find by following coordinates posted on the internet.

WHO GOES THERE Social folks who like to play outdoor games and enjoy a bonfire pit with other tiny home dwellers.

COST A lot leases for $450/month; tiny homes range from $70,000–$80,000.

CONTACT 976 Geer Hwy., Travelers Rest, SC 29690 **Phone** 313-444-4140 **Web** creekwalkcommunity.com

THE GIANT BOOK OF TINY HOMES

Stay at this Wisconsin tiny house in the autumn, when colors are outrageous and summer's swelter is gone.

Canoe Bay Escape Village
Chetek, Wisconsin

LOCATION Northwest Wisconsin, on more than 100 acres of hardwood forests, wetlands and private lakes.

FEATURES An "escape village" with fully furnished one-bedroom and two-bedroom tiny homes, many with wetlands or lake views. Each house includes a Keurig machine, flat-screen TV and well-equipped wet bar. If you stay for a night and love it, you can buy a tiny home and lease a site.

WHO GOES THERE Tiny home fans who want to enjoy lounging on a screened porch "while listening to seasonal wildlife and taking in the fresh air…," says the website.

COST $295/night.

CONTACT 1740 20½ St., Rice Lake, WI 54868 **Phone** 844-696-3722 **Web** escapevillages.com

🏠 THE TINY HOME LIFE

Getaway rentals are ideal for those who prefer peace and quiet—and disconnecting from digital devices.

Getaway Cabins Nationwide

LOCATION Getaway retreats are located within driving distance of several major cities (including Boston, New York, Washington and Los Angeles) on 11 sites, with more to come. In keeping with Getaway's in-the-moment ethos, visitors get the exact address of their rental only one week before a planned vacation.
FEATURES Just nature and a two- or four-person tiny home with the basics. Getaway tiny homes are nestled in unspoiled wilderness meant to help guests disconnect and recharge. Tiny houses—from 160 to 200 square feet—include a cellphone lockbox (they're serious about disconnecting), board games, classic books and a guide to "analog" activities like knot-tying and stargazing.
WHO GOES THERE People who are serious about simplicity. Homes have no Wi-Fi or TVs, so if you can't live without digital connections, stay somewhere else.
COST $125–$150/night.
CONTACT 147 Prince St., Brooklyn, NY 11201 **Phone** 617-914-0021 **Web** getaway.house

Ask about Caravan's regular home tours that give you info on tiny-house building and living.

Caravan
Portland, Oregon

LOCATION In the heart of the Alberta Arts District in Portland, steps from foodie havens, galleries and tattoo parlors.

FEATURES A "Portlandia" experience of six custom-built tiny houses (one looks like a train caboose) that form a circle to create a central gathering space with BBQ, fire pit and local art. "Best of all, we offer all-you-can-eat s'mores with vegan marshmallows, organic graham crackers (including optional gluten-free graham crackers) and Fair Trade dark and milk chocolate!" the website says.

WHO GOES THERE Foodies and gallery-hoppers who want to vacation in a tiny home located in a vibrant, urban location. Although city noises are muted by gratis earplugs and a high-end white-noise machine in each home, light sleepers may not find this tiny home experience a good fit for them.

COST $165–$175/night, based on two-person occupancy.

CONTACT 5009 NE 11th Ave., Portland, OR 97211 **Phone** 503-288-5225 **Web** tinyhousehotel.com

🏠 THE TINY HOME LIFE

Decorative lattice skirting and a colorful staircase bring a dash of Florida chic to this lakeside cottage.

Orlando Lakefront at College Park
Orlando, Florida

LOCATION Seven minutes from downtown Orlando and 20 minutes from theme parks and attractions.
FEATURES This established RV park, which offers boat and fishing docks on Lake Fairview, is growing tiny organically: As RVs leave, spaces go to tiny homes on wheels or foundations. Bring your own home, or rent one.
WHO GOES THERE Disney lovers and other tiny-homers who like warm weather and lakeside living close to a thriving downtown.
COST Lot leases range from $350–$550/month.
CONTACT 3405 N. Orange Blossom Trail, Orlando, FL 32804 **Phone** 407-936-4094 **Web** orlandolakefrontth.com

Village Farm Tiny Home Community, Austin, Texas

LOCATION An "agri-hood" in East Austin, Texas.
FEATURES A sustainable community of turnkey tiny homes with a working farm, trails, pool, fitness center and farmers market.
WHO GOES THERE Community-spirited folks who want to enjoy an outdoor amphitheater, community center and collaborative work space while reducing their carbon footprint.
COST $60,000–$150,000 for 400-square-foot homes (one-bedroom or one-bedroom-plus-loft models available).
CONTACT 8207 Canoga Ave., Austin, TX 78724
Phone 512-995-7335
Web villagefarmaustin.com

Generous covered porches increase the available living area.

Tiny Facts

The Tiny Life website (thetinylife.com) conducted a survey of tiny-house dwellers and uncovered these interesting stats:

- 64.1% are female

- 45% range from 22 to 40 years old

- Tiny-house people are more likely to hold college or graduate degrees than the average U.S. person

- The household income of tiny home dwellers, which had topped the typical U.S. household, has been dropping to slightly lower

INDEX

A
Accessory dwelling unit (ADU), 11
 in Ashville, North Carolina, 46–51
Air conditioner, 18
Aladdin kit home company, 71
American National Standards Institute (ANSI) 119.5, 22
Ashland, Oregon, cottage in, 72–77
Ashville, North Carolina, accessory dwelling unit in, 46–51

B
Backsplashes, 35
Baldwin, Emory. *See* FabCab
Bathroom vanities, clearance requirements, 38
Bathrooms, 36–39
Bathtub, soaking tub vs., 39
Body-care products, homemade, 58
British Columbia, off-grid cabin in, 152–157
Brown, Teal. *See* Wishbone Tiny Homes
Budget, assessing your, 17
Budget considerations, 17
Buildable footprint, lot size vs., 74–75
Building codes, 22–23
 bathrooms, 37, 38
 local regulations, 18, 37
 outhouses, 170
 in rural locations, 78
Bump-outs, 46, 75

C
Cabins
 Lake Pend Oreille, Idaho, 120–121, 134–139
 Methow Valley, Washington, 144–151
 prefabricated, in New Hampshire, 78–85
 remote off-grid, 152–157
 rustic, from salvaged material, 128–133
 San Juan Island, Washington, 140–143
 treehouses, 122–127
California, cottages in, 52–59, 86–91
Campbell, Erika and Tish, 108–113
Canoe Bay Escape Village, Wisconsin, 181
Caravan, Portland, Oregon, 183
Ceilings, high, 18
Challenges, 107
Charleston, South Carolina, DIY tiny house in, 114–119
Children, tiny lifestyle with, 24–29, 114–119
Cleaning products, homemade, 57
Collins, Clark, 1940s cottage restoration by, 86–91
Compost bin, 59
Compostable toilet, 170
Concrete flooring, 81–83
Concrete slab foundation, 44–51, 82–83
Cottages
 in Ashland, Oregon, 72–77
 farmhouse-style, in Texas Hill Country, 66–71
 Maine oceanside getaway, 60–65
 restored 1940s, in Laguna Beach, California, 86–91
 in Venice Beach, California, 52–59
Countertops, 35, 83
Cowboy Cabin, 128–133
Craftsman cottage, in Venice Beach, California, 52–59
Creek Walk Tiny Home Community, South Carolina, 180
creekwalkcommunity.com, 180
Custom cabinetry, maximizing space with, 35

D
Delgado, Carlos (architect), 74–76
Design features, increasing space perception, 18
Digital Tiny House Workshop, 113
Dinner party, tips on throwing, 164–167
Do-it-yourself (DIY) tiny homes, 108–119
 plan costs, 114
Doors, sliding, 149, 151
 barn-like, 38, 42–43, 65, 84, 110, 118
 pocket, 38
 storage space above, 41
Downsizing, 7, 17
 benefits of, 107
 strategies, 98
Drying rack, 53

E
Eagle Point cabin, San Juan Island, Washington, 140–143
Electric current, DC vs. AC, 172–173
Electric mini-split heater/air conditioner, 18, 175

Energy costs/Energy efficiency, 2, 28, 55, 143, 172, 175, 176
   solar access and, 77
Energy recovery ventilator (ERV), 82
Entertaining, small-scale, 164–167
Environmentally friendly Craftsman cottage, in Venice Beach, California, 52–59
escapevillages.com, 181

F

FabCab (prefabricated homes), 80–81, 82
Family-friendly tiny houses
   in Charleston, South Carolina, 114–119
   reflections on living in, 24–29
Farmhouse-style cottage, in Hill Country, Texas, 66–71
Financial issues, 7
Flat tire, changing, 104
"Flatpack" (panel-built) houses, 14
Floor plans
   10-sided cabin, 120–121, 134–139
   accessory dwelling unit, 48
   Methow Valley cabin, 148
   off-grid cabin, 154
   prefabricated cabin, 80
Florida, tiny house community in, 184
Freeport, Maine, oceanside getaway cottage in, 60–65
Furnishings, multifunctional, 18

G

Galley kitchens, 26, 29, 43, 89, 96, 142
Garden, planning and planting, 162–163
Gardner, Tracen. *See* Reclaimed Space (construction company)
Getaway cabins/Getaway cottages, 11, 15, 60–65, 78–85, 144–151
   nationwide rentals/leased lots, 178–185
   off-grid, 152–157
   of 1940s California, 86–91
getaway.house, 182
Golden Rule Construction company, 136
Granny pods, 12–13

H

Habitable space, NASA calculations vs. typical tiny house, 18
Hammer, Martin, 22

Heat recovery ventilator (HRV), 82
Heating/Heaters, 175–177
   mini-split heater/air conditioners, 18, 175
   underfloor, 38
Hill Country, Texas, farmhouse-style cottage in, 66–71
Holding tank, for water supply, 174
Homes/Houses, examples by size. *See* Square footage
Hooks, 42
Horseshoe kitchen, 32–33, 63
Hulbert, Chuck and Pam, 135–136, 139

I

Idaho, 10-sided cabin in, 120–121, 134–139
Incinerating toilet, 170
Indoor plants
   best for small spaces, 160–161
   decorating with, 54–59
Insulation, 7, 18, 55, 80, 142, 174–175, 176–177
International Residential Code (IRC), 18
"2018 IRC Appendix Q, Tiny Houses" (Morrison & Hammer), 22

J

Johnston, Mary and Ray (architects), 146, 148–150

K

Kettle River Timberworks, 156
   off-grid construction details, 157
Kingwell, Brian, 154, 156
Kitchen appliances/equipment, 33–35
   energy-efficient, 172
   hand-operated, 42
   solar power considerations, 172–173
Kitchen islands, 82, 146, 148
   adaptable/movable, 35
Kitchen planning
   priorities, 30–35
   windows in, 30
Kittel, Darby, 131, 132

L

Laguna Beach, California, restored 1940s cottage in, 86–91
Leavenworth Tiny House Village, Washington, 178–179

187

INDEX

leavenworthtinyhouse.com/home, 179
Life lessons, tiny house, 107
Living roofs
  how to make, 139
  Lake Pend Oreille, Idaho, 120–121, 134–139
  San Juan Island, Washington, 140–143
Living space, outdoor. See Outdoor space, as living space
Local regulations, building/zoning, 18
  outhouses, 170
Loft staircases, 84, 98, 102
  shelves combined with, 132
  storage under, 44, 111, 116
  utilizing space under, 33
Lot size, buildable footprint vs., 74–75

M

Maine, oceanside getaway cottage in, 60–65
Manufactured housing, 12
  tiny houses vs., 23
Methow Valley, Washington, cabin in, 144–151
Miller, Macy (blogger), on living tiny, 108
  with children, 24–29
Mini-split heater/air conditioner, 18, 175
Minimalism, 107, 115
Mobile homes, 12
Modular houses, 12
Morris, Whitney Leigh, 52–59
Morrison, Andrew, 22
Motor home. See Recreational vehicles (RVs)
Multifunctional furnishings, 18, 98
Multipurpose rooms, 59

N

National Fire Protection Association (NFPA) 1192, 22
National Kitchen & Bath Association (NKBA), 36
Nelson, Pete, on treehouses, 122–126
Nelson Island, British Columbia, off-grid cabin on, 152–157
Nelson Treehouse and Supply (construction company), 127
nelsontreehouse.com/treehouseresortandspa, 126

New Hampshire, prefabricated cabin in, 78–85

O

Off-grid construction, 157
Off-grid houses
  challenges and rewards of, 152–157
  heating issues, 168, 174–175, 176–177
  solar power for, 171–173
  toilet options, 170
  water source/supply for, 173, 174
Olsen, Lorraine, 72–77
Oregon
  cottage in Ashland, 72–77
  DIY tiny house in Portland, 108–113
  tiny house community in Portland, 183
Orlando Lakefront at College Park, Florida, 184
orlandolakefrontth.com, 184
Outdoor space, as living space
  decks, 18–19
  porches, 18, 49, 81, 130, 185
Outhouse, 170
Owens, Eric, 135

P

Panel-built houses, 14
Parenting, living tiny and, 29
Park model, 23
Pate, Chris and Sheradan, 115–119
Petrina, Dave. See Kettle River Timberworks
Picard Point, Lake Pend Oreille, Idaho, 120–121, 134–139
Plants. See also Indoor plants
  for living roof, 138–139
  for raised garden beds, 162–163
Plastic kitchenwares, 57
Porches, 18, 49, 81, 130, 185
Portland, Oregon
  DIY tiny house in, 108–113
  tiny house community in, 183
Prefab housing, 14
Prefabulous Small Houses (Koones), 84
Prentiss Balance Wickline Architects, 140
Pressure tank, for water supply, 174
Propane heaters, 176–177
Propane stoves, 175

Q
Quality time, 7, 27

R
Rainbow Row, Charleston, South Carolina, 116
Raised garden beds, 162–163
Reclaimed/Recycled materials
  for farmhouse-style cottage, 66–71
  for rustic Cowboy Cabin, 128–133
Reclaimed Space (construction company), 66–77
Recreational Vehicle Industry Association (RVIA), 23
Recreational vehicles (RVs). See also Tiny house RV; Tiny houses on wheels (THOWs)
  classifications, 15
  terminology, 14
  tiny houses vs., 23
Regulations. See Building codes; Zoning ordinances
Relationships, living tiny and, 27
Remote construction. See Off-grid houses
Rentals, getaway cabins, 182
Residential zones/codes, 11, 15, 22, 37, 113. See also International Residential Code (IRC)
Roofs. See Living roofs; Shed-style roofs

S
Salvage Texas community, 132
Salvaged materials. See Reclaimed/Recycled materials
San Juan Island, Washington, cabin on, 140–143
Saving money, 7, 28
Secondhand items, 58
Septic system, 170
Shed-style roofs, 46, 116, 140–141, 147, 148
Shelving, 41, 42
  and loft staircase combination, 132
Showers, 37, 38–39
  outdoor, 58
Single-use disposable products, 57
Skylights, 18, 111, 156
Sleeping lofts, 51, 80, 85, 102–103, 118–119, 131, 133
Small-scale entertaining, 164–167

Soaking tub, bathtub vs., 39
Sofa bed, built-in, 59
Solar access, described, 77
Solar power, 171–173
Solid foundations, concrete-slab, 44–51, 82–83
South Carolina
  Charleston DIY family friendly house, 114–119
  tiny house community in, 180
Space. See also Square footage
  buildable footprint, lot size vs., 74–75
  bump-outs and, 46, 75
  empty, appreciating, 107
  hand-operated appliances and, 42
  maximizing, 18, 35
  overall size considerations, 18
Spare time, 7, 27
Spesard, Jenna (tiny house traveler), 100–107
Square footage, house examples
  <400 square foot (tiny houses), 24–29, 46–51, 94–119, 122–126, 128–133
  400–1,000 square foot (small houses), 52–91, 134–157
Staircases. See Loft staircases
Statistics, tiny house dwellers, 185
Steel rods, for kitchen utensils, 35, 42
Storage, ideas for, 40–43, 97, 113
  under loft staircases, 44, 111
Structurally insulated panels (SIPs), 80, 176–177
Succession planting, 163

T
Texas
  Hill Country farmhouse-style cottage, 66–71
  tiny house communities in, 132, 185
Time-savers, tiny houses as, 7, 27
Tiny house communities, 132, 178–185
Tiny-house dwellers, statistics on, 18
Tiny house RV
  building codes, 22–23
  tiny house vs., 23
  zoning ordinances, 23
Tiny houses (less than 400 square foot), examples, 24–29, 46–51, 94–119, 122–126, 128–133

INDEX

Tiny houses on wheels (THOWs)
  building codes, 22
  legal issues, 15, 22–23
  zoning ordinances, 22
Tiny Texas Houses (building company), 131
tinycanalcottage.com, 53
tinyhousebuild.com, 111, 113
tinyhousegiantjourney.com, 104
tinyhousehotel.com, 183
Toilets
  clearance requirements, 37
  for off-grid houses, 170
Towing costs, 103, 104
Toybox Tiny Home, 94–95
Trailer platforms, tiny homes built on, 92–119
  changing flat tire, 104
Traveling, with tiny houses, 100–107
Treehouses, 122–127
"2018 IRC Appendix Q: Tiny Houses" (Morrison & Hammer), 22

U
Upgrading strategies, 98

V
Vegetables, growing in raised beds, 162–163
Venice Beach, California, Craftsman cottage in, 52–59
Vertone, Janine, 154
Village Farm Tiny Home Community, Texas, 185
villagefarmaustin.com, 184

W
Wall-rack system, 41
Washer/dryer combo, 33
Washington state
  cabins in, 140–151
  tiny house community in, 178–179
Water heaters, tankless, 37
Water pipes, winterizing, 176–177
Water source/supply, for off-grid house, 173, 174
Watson, Jesse (builder), 136
Wells/Well pumps, 173–174
Wicker baskets, 42
Windows, 18
  in kitchen, 30
  salvaged, 130–131
Winterizing your tiny home, 176–177
Wisconsin, tiny house community in, 181
Wishbone Tiny Homes, 47–48
Wood stoves, 175, 176

Z
Zoning ordinances, 22
  local regulations, 18
  outhouses, 170

CREDITS

COVER Irvin Serrano **2-3** Thousand Trails & Encore RV Resorts & Campgrounds **4-5** Sean Bagshaw; Woods Wheatcroft; Mieke Zuiderweg; Whitney Leigh Morris/Tiny Canal Cottage **6-7** TT/IStock/Getty Images **8-9** Ross Chapin Architects **10-11** thebearwalk.com **12-13** Jamie Hooper/Shutterstock **14-15** ppa/Shutterstock; Art Roderick Aichinger **16-17** thebearwalk.com **18-19** Dylan Jon Wade Cox; Courtesy of MyBox **20-21** Roderick Aichinger **22-23** Michelle Solobay; Ball & Albanese **24-25** Macy Miller/MiniMotives.com (2) **26-27** Macy Miller/MiniMotives.com (2) **28-29** Macy Miller/MiniMotives.com (2) **30-31** Michaela Klenkove/Shutterstock **32-33** Courtesy of Loud TV **34-35** Roderick Aichinger/Getaway; Dmitry Galaganov/Shutterstock **36-37** Photographee.eu/Shutterstock; thebearwalk.com (2) **38-39** ppa/Shutterstock; Mieke Zuiderweg; Dariusz Jarzabek/Shutterstock **40-41** Tria Giovan/GAP Interiors; Colin Poole/GAP Interiors **42-43** Bilanol/Shutterstock; ppa/Shutterstock **44-45** Astrid Hinderks/Alamy Stock Photo **46-47** Deborah Scannell (2) **48-49** Deborah Scannell (2) **50-51** Deborah Scannell (2) **52-53** Whitney Leigh Morris/Tiny Canal Cottage (2) **54-55** Whitney Leigh Morris/Tiny Canal Cottage (4) **56-57** Whitney Leigh Morris/Tiny Canal Cottage (2) **58-59** Whitney Leigh Morris/Tiny Canal Cottage (6) **60-61** Irvin Serrano **62-63** Irvin Serrano (3) **64-65** Irvin Serrano (2) **66-67** Reclaimed Space **68-69** Reclaimed Space (3) **70-71** Reclaimed Space (3) **72-73** Sean Bagshaw **74-75** Sean Bagshaw (2) **76-77** Sean Bagshaw (3) **78-79** Jim Mauchly (2) **80-81** Jim Mauchly (3) **82-83** Jim Mauchly (2) **84-85** Jim Mauchly (4) **86-87** Grey Crawford (2) **88-89** Grey Crawford (3) **90-91** Grey Crawford (4) **92-93** Chris Pate **94-95** Mieke Zuiderweg **96-97** Mieke Zuiderweg (2) **98-99** Mieke Zuiderweg (3) **100-101** Guillaume Dutilh **102-103** Guillaume Dutilh (4) **104-105** Guillaume Dutilh (4) **106-107** Guillaume Dutilh **108-109** John Riha (2) **110-111** John Riha (3); Erika Campbell (2) **112-113** John Riha (3) **114-115** Chris Pate (2) **116-117** Chris Pate (2); Gordon Bell/Shutterstock **118-119** Chris Pate (3) **120-121** Woods Wheatcroft **122-123** Nelson Treehouse & Supply (2) **124-125** Nelson Treehouse & Supply (3) **126-127** Nelson Treehouse & Supply (6) **128-129** Jeff Harris (2) **130-131** Jeff Harris (3) **132-133** Jeff Harris (4) **134-135** Woods Wheatcroft **136-137** Woods Wheatcroft (4) **138-139** Woods Wheatcroft (2) **140-141** Adam Michael Waldo (2) **142-143** Adam Michael Waldo (5) **144-145** Will Austin/Johnston Architects **146-147** Will Austin/Johnston Architects (3) **148-149** Will Austin/Johnston Architects (2) **150-151** Will Austin/Johnston Architects (3) **152-153** Dom Koric Photography **154-155** Dom Koric Photography (3); Tim Sheridan **156-157** Dom Koric Photography (4) **158-159** Ross Chapin Architects **160-161** rattiya lamrod/Shutterstock **162-163** Alexander Raths/Shutterstock; Dave Toht/Rebecca Anderson; Eag1eEyes/Shutterstock; amenic181/Shutterstock **164-165** Jack Frog/Shutterstock **166-167** REDA&CO/Getty Images; Jack Frog/Shutterstock **168-169** Ariel Celeste Photography/Shutterstock; Estrada Anton/Shutterstock **170-171** Fotokon/Shutterstock; salajean/Shutterstock **172-173** Ariel Celeste Photography/Shutterstock; I am a Stranger/Shutterstock **174-175** DyziO/Shutterstock; bearwalk.com **176-177** Pine and Palms Journal; thebearwalk.com **178-179** Courtesy of Leavenworth Tiny House Village (2) **180-181** Courtesy of Creek Walk Community (4); Courtesy of Canoe Bay Escape Village (4) **182-183** Courtesy of Getway Cabins (3); Courtesy of Caravan Portland (3) **184-185** Courtesy of Orlando Lakefront at College Park (2); Courtesy of Village Farm Tiny Home Community (3) **BACK COVER** Will Austin/Johnston Architects

SPECIAL THANKS TO CONTRIBUTING WRITERS

Stacy Freed, Lisa Kaplan Gordon, Macy Miller, Whitney Leigh Morris, Andrew Morrison, Jenna Spesard, Deidre Sullivan, Michelle Tascione, Dave Toht, Jan Soults Walker

CENTENNIAL BOOKS

An Imprint of
Centennial Media, LLC
40 Worth St., 10th Floor
New York, NY 10013, U.S.A.

CENTENNIAL BOOKS is a trademark of Centennial Media, LLC

All rights reserved. No part of this publication may be reproduced, stored in a retrieval system, or transmitted in any form or by any means (including electronic, mechanical, photocopying, recording, or otherwise) without prior written permission from the publisher.

ISBN 978-1-951274-53-5

Distributed by
Simon & Schuster, Inc.
1230 Avenue of the Americas
New York, NY 10020, U.S.A.

For information about custom editions, special sales and premium and corporate purchases, please contact Centennial Media at contact@centennialmedia.com.

Manufactured in China

© 2021 by Centennial Media, LLC

10 9 8 7 6 5 4 3 2 1

Publishers & Co-Founders Ben Harris, Sebastian Raatz
Editorial Director Annabel Vered
Creative Director Jessica Power
Executive Editor Janet Giovanelli
Deputy Editors Ron Kelly, Alyssa Shaffer
Design Director Martin Elfers
Senior Art Director Pino Impastato
Art Directors Olga Jakim, Natali Suasnavas, Joseph Ulatowski
Copy/Production Patty Carroll, Angela Taormina
Assistant Art Director Jaclyn Loney
Photo Editor Jenny Veiga
Production Manager Paul Rodina
Production Assistant Alyssa Swiderski
Editorial Assistant Tiana Schippa
Sales & Marketing Jeremy Nurnberg